The Canadian Guide to American DO Medical Schools & International Medical Education
2017 edition

ISBN: 0995893500
ISBN-13: 978-0995893504

Dedicated to the memory of Dr. Fiddler D.O., who kept the flame of osteopathic medicine alive in Canada

"A toast, to absent friends, in memory still bright"

Table of contents

List of Abbreviations

AACOM - The American Association of Colleges of Osteopathic Medicine
ABFM - The American Board of Family Medicine
ACGME - The Accreditation Council for Graduate Medical Education
AMCAS - The American Medical College Application Service
AMG - American medical graduate (anyone who has graduated from an American medical school, MD or DO)
AOA - The American Osteopathic Association
CACMS - The Committee on Accreditation of Canadian Medical Schools
CaRMS - The Canadian Resident Matching Service
CEGEP - Collège d'enseignement général et professionnel / General and Vocational College. A publically funded pre-university college in Quebec.
CFPC - The College of Family Physicians of Canada
CMG - Canadian medical graduate (anyone who has graduated from a Canadian medical school)
COA - The Canadian Osteopathic Association
COCA - The Commission on Osteopathic College Accreditation
COMSA - The Canadian Osteopathic Medical Student Association
COMLEX - The Comprehensive Osteopathic Medical Licensing Examination
cGPA - cumulative grade point average
CSA - Canadian(s) studying abroad. A CSA becomes an IMG upon graduation.
DO - Doctor of osteopathic medicine
ERAS - Electronic Residency Application Service (The American residency matching service)
FPMRAC - Federation of Medical Regulatory Authorities of Canada
FREIDA - A free database of ACGME accredited residencies and fellowships
GME - Graduate medical education
GPA - grade point average

IMG - International medical graduate (anyone who has graduated from a medical school outside of the US or Canada).
IP - In province
LMCE - The Liaison Committee on Medical Education
MBBS - Bachelor of Medicine, Bachelor of Surgery (A medical degree granted by most common-wealth countries)
MCAT - The Medical College Admission Test
MCC - The Medical Council of Canada
MCCEE - The Medical Council of Canada Evaluation Exam
MCCQE I - The Medical Council of Canada Qualifying exam Part 1
MCCQE II - The Medical Council of Canada Qualifying exam part II
MD - Doctor of allopathic medicine
MLK - Martin Luther King day
NAC OSCE - National Assessment Collaboration (**NAC**) Objective Structured Clinical Examination (**OSCE**)
NRMP - The National Resident Matching Program
OMSAS - Ontario Medical School Application Service
OMM - Osteopathic Manipulative Medicine
OMT - Osteopathic Manipulative Treatment
OOP - Out of province
OPT - Optional practical training
SDN - Student doctor network, an online forum
SWOMEN - South-western Ontario Medical Education Network
USDO - US trained doctor of osteopathic medicine
USMD - US trained doctor of allopathic medicine
USMLE - United States Medical Licensing Exam
UofT - University of Toronto
UWORLD - USMLE World, an online test bank service
VSAS - Visiting Student Application Service

Prologue

How to use this book

This book is divided into part one and part two. Part one deals with the issues facing undergraduate pre-medical students and the background information they need to succeed in today's Canadian and American entrance requirements to the medical profession.

Part two is tailored towards medical students and gives them a practical to-the-point guide of the common pitfalls, strategies and views they should have in order to maximize their success in the competitive world of medical education.

For the undergraduate pre-med, it is recommended that they read part one thoroughly, as that is everything they need to know to make the right decision for medical education. For the medical student, they are suggested to skip over to part two as they should already be quite familiar with the information outlined in part one. The information in part two should be much more relevant to them.

You will see various **experiential pearls** sections: these are personal experiences of the things I have done, or the things I have seen other people do. Hopefully, you will find these anecdotes helpful to yourself during this long process or at the very least, make for an entertaining read.

The framework you need for success

I was born in 1986 in the People's Republic of China. I left China with my parents when I was seven years old. We first moved to Belgium where we stayed for five years. There, I attended St. John's International School in Waterloo, where I learned English and was exposed to international pupils from all over the world.

My parents and I left Belgium and immigrated to Canada in 1997. Toronto is where my family settled.

I graduated from the Danforth Collegiate and Technical Institute of the Toronto district school board. I completed my Honors Bachelor of Science with a major in human biology, and minors in biology and anthropology at the University of Toronto, St. George campus. I then completed my Doctor of Osteopathic Medicine (D.O.) at Western University of Health Sciences - College of Osteopathic Medicine of the Pacific in Pomona, California in June 2014. I matched and returned home to Canada to start my residency training in family medicine at McMaster University, Brampton site. I completed my residency training in 2016, and started a family medicine practice in Aurora, Ontario, Canada.

Having travelled greatly, and having lived on three different continents, I was exposed to many different political, economic and educational systems. From my experiences, I have acquired **two** simple principles which I use to make decisions and to plan goals in my life.

(One) Get to the highest position possible, in the shortest amount of time.
(Two) Seek truth from facts

These two are my mantra, and the strategy outlined in this book will come from this perspective.

Let me explain. For principle one, we live in a capitalist society, and as an individual living in such a society, you want to get to the highest position possible, in the shortest amount of time. Success is maximizing the results, minimizing the effort, and to attain the greatest in the least amount of time. For instance, after a few years delay, a large number of the people in my graduation year eventually made it into medical school in Canada. However, the problem was that they were four years behind me in their medical careers. I had finished medical school, started residency and they had just began. In my mind, that is four years of lost revenue as a physician. You can multiply the number of years they were behind me (i.e. 4 years) by $200,000 a year (i.e., a low to medium estimate of the revenue of a starting physician right after family medicine residency in Canada) and come up with an estimate of their lost income. This is why I would always strongly encourage someone to start and finish medical school early in life, as opposed to later in life.

For principle two, one should investigate and study the facts of your specific task or locality, and base your policy and actions on that. Do not start from preconceived "truths" and amass the facts to prove yourself right, while neglecting facts that cast doubt on your conclusions.

The first two principles have carried me far in life, and I hope that you, as the reader, will be able to learn something from my journey.

"act in the world as it is, and not in the world as we wish it were."

- Henry Stimson

Introduction

Section 1: The reality of entrance to medical education in Canada

Did you know that your chance of going to medical school in Canada is strongly affected by the geographical location in which you grew up or went to school?

Did you know that there is a huge difference between applying as an **out-of-province (OOP)** applicant compared to an **in-province (IP)** applicant?

Did you know that your cGPA, MCAT or hard statistics don't need to be nearly as high if you are an in-province applicant compared to an out-of-province applicant?

Did you know that there is a game being played by pre-meds who know the rules and try to establish residence in a certain province as a way to improve their chances of matriculating into a medical school in Canada?

Did you know that the success rate of medical school acceptance is only 20% or less in Canada?

Let me explain.

Acceptance into a Canadian medical school is a very difficult process. Take the province of Ontario for instance, in the 2016 application cycle; there are **961 projected seats** for the 2017 entering class and **6,476 individual applicants** for those spots (1). This translates into a **14.8% acceptance rate** for medical schools in Ontario.

Year after year, countless individuals are refused an interview or fail to matriculate after multiple application cycles due to the competitive nature of the process. Because of the fierce competition, many people are forced to give up on the career path of medicine, or to go back to school for a second undergrad, or a graduate degree in attempts to bolster their credentials for re-application to medical school. Unfortunately, many qualified individuals are unable to obtain a seat in medical school in Canada, and are forced to pursue a different career, or to go overseas for international medical education.

Added on top of the general difficulty of medical school acceptance in Canada is the issue of the **different standards set in the different provinces of what constitutes a competitive candidate**. You see, entrance requirements in the different provinces across Canada are far from uniform. Depending on your province of residence, there are wildly different cut-offs and statistics required for a successful interview invitation or acceptance to medical school. With the exception of Ontario, all other provinces in Canada distinguish applicants to their medical schools based on geographical location. Those who had lived for some time in those provinces will apply under the category of an "In-Province" (IP) applicant. Those who are applying from another province, or had not lived a part of their lives in the province in which they are applying, will fall under the category of an "out-of-province" (OOP) applicant.

To be an OOP applicant is to be at a significant disadvantage. The provinces usually allocate a very small number of seats in their medical programs for successful matriculants who are out-of-province. For example, at the University of British Columbia medical school for the 2016 entrance year, of the 288 available spots, only up to 10% or 29 seats are reserved for OOP applicants, of which 20 were actual OOP matriculants for that year (2). IP applicants have a minimum cGPA cut off of 75%, whereas OOP applicants have to meet an 85% minimum cGPA cut off (3).

Similarly, at Memorial University medical school, of the 80-84 seats available each year, only 5 are reserved for non-maritime provinces, non-Yukon applicants as well as non-Canadians, while 57 seats are reserved for residents of Newfoundland and Labrador. There were 200 IP applicants for the 57 seats reserved for residents of Newfoundland and Labrador, whereas 350 people competed for the 5 seats reserved for non-maritime provinces, non-Yukon applicants (4). Because of these small numbers of positions, the competition for them is fierce.

Take the University of Manitoba as another example. On their website, for the class of 2020, you can see that the IP matriculant had both a lower average cGPA and MCAT than an OOP applicant. Specifically, the accepted Manitoba pool had an average GPA of 4.03 (on a 4.5 scale) and average MCAT of 9.95 (or 506 on the new MCAT), while the OOP pool's average GPA was 4.22 with an average MCAT of 11.20 (or 523 on the new MCAT) (5). You can see this similar trend across the years.

Similar examples can be found across the provinces in Canada. UBC, McGill, University of Manitoba (to name a few) all have higher cut-offs and standards for applicants who are out-of-province compared to applicants who come in-province. If you still don't believe me, you can easily visit the websites of other Canadian medical schools and see for yourself.

What we have here is a system where geography plays a significant role, instead of a system that is based on absolute merit. In some aspects, it really is protectionism of the provinces to medical school entrance. Aside from the role that geography plays in the entrance selection process, some provinces simply have an easier path to medical school. For example, Quebec's medical schools accept applicants after a two-year **CEGEP diploma**, which is the equivalent of other provinces' grade 12 plus the first year of university. I have been told that half of the seats in Quebec's medical schools are filled by graduates of the CEGEP diploma - meaning they were accepted to medical school on what would effectively be grade 12 and the first year of undergraduate studies in the other provinces. If you were a pre-med who was not a resident of Quebec, I would imagine that it hardly seems fair that the rest of Canada requires the pre-med to have at least three years of undergraduate studies completed under their belt before they can matriculate in a medical school, and most people have completed at least a 4 year bachelor's program before matriculating in a medical school. Unfortunately, this is the country we live in, and we must adapt to this system in order to succeed.

Medicine is one of the most sought after professions in Canada. Aside from the prestige of being physicians, medicine is a recession proof profession. Being in the medical profession in Canada will basically guarantee a lifestyle that the majority of people can only dream about. Given that everyone has a drive for a sound financial future and given the general difficulty of acceptance to a Canadian medical program, pre-meds who are well versed in the process of medical school application have figured out ways to improve their odds of acceptance to medical school.

A common tactic is to obtain in-province status by becoming a resident of a province in which they wish to apply for medical school. A popular destination is Alberta, as only twelve months of presence in that province would make you a resident of Alberta. I have personally come across examples of people becoming residents of provinces (through one way or another) in which they hoped to go for medical school as a way to enter the category of the "in-province" applicant pool.

One must understand that applying as an IP candidate is much easier than an OOP candidate. I once knew a person who was a resident of Ontario, who was fluent in French and wanted to attend McGill for medical school. This person did attend McGill for undergrad, but the rules at the time stated that going to university in Quebec was not an acceptable criterion to becoming a resident of Quebec. At the time, McGill had a quota of ten spots for their entering class that was reserved for applicants outside of Quebec. You can imagine that the competition for the ten reserved spots was fiercely competitive. My friend applied as an OOP candidate to McGill, and unfortunately was unsuccessful in obtaining one of the ten spots. This is when everything became more dubious. This individual had several relatives living in Quebec who were Quebec residents. Through various means, this person was able to obtain Quebec residence with help from their relatives, through various old utilities bill statements and bank statements. My friend applied a second time as an IP candidate to McGill, and was subsequently accepted.

A similar story happened with another friend of mine who is a resident of Manitoba. I have known this person throughout undergrad at the University of Toronto. Their cGPA was around a mid to high 3.60, and their MCAT was a rounded 31R (~510), these stats was fairly average at the time. Look at the average GPA and MCAT for successful medical school matriculants in Ontario. You can go on University of Toronto's website and see the average MCAT, cGPA score of matriculants for the last several years. When the average entrance cGPA is as high as 3.89, a mid to high 3.60 is nothing special. This individual applied for multiple cycles in Ontario but did not receive any interview invitations. This person was not aware of the in-province and out-of-province distinction at the time, but eventually figured it out and applied to both Manitoba and Ontario during their last application cycle. This individual still did not receive any interviews in Ontario, but applied as an in-province candidate in Manitoba, and was invited to interview in their home province and was subsequently accepted.

Due to IP status, a 3.6-3.7 cGPA (on a 4.0 scale) with 30s/509 MCAT may be enough to matriculate in Manitoba, but an applicant from Ontario or another province with equal statistics will not even receive an interview invitation. In order to have a good chance of acceptance as an out-of-province applicant in Manitoba, the applicant would have to be more qualified with almost a 3.9 cGPA and 35/517 and above MCAT. Similar statements can be made for other provinces like British Columbia, Alberta, and the Maritime Provinces.

Another friend happened to have married a spouse who was a resident of Newfoundland (from family ties). By virtue of their spouse, they also became a resident of Newfoundland despite the fact that they had never previously set foot on Newfoundland, and have no other ties to Newfoundland except through their extended in-laws. Initially, this individual did not have aspirations for medical school during undergrad, but after a few years in the workforce, and after getting laid off in their industry, this individual changed their mind, took the MCAT and decided to pursue medicine. This individual's grades did not secure any interviews in Ontario, but managed to obtain an interview at Memorial University through the IP stream (a common theme it seems!), and as a resident of Newfoundland no less. This person was accepted through the IP stream at Memorial, and the rest was history.

A lot can be learned from the three stories I illustrated above. First, pre-meds can be quite ingenious when it comes to playing the game, and getting medical school acceptance in Canada. Second, in order to succeed in the current medical school entrance climate, one must be aware of these tricks.

The three examples I mentioned above should illustrate that the standards for admission is drastically different depending on your geographical location, and whether you have IP access. It is an unfair system and the sooner the pre-med recognizes this, the better they will be prepared for this game.

This system is unfair in the sense that people with IP status require lower stats to be granted a chance at medical school admission. It is unfair in that one's future can be dictated based on geographical destiny, as opposed to a true meritocracy. Unfortunately, protectionism of medical school entrance exists at the provincial level in Canada.

On this same token, a pre-med in Ontario is at a major disadvantage compared to pre-meds in other provinces. You see, unlike the other provinces, Ontario for the most part does not have in-province or out-of-province distinction during the application process. There are Ontario schools like Western who have a preference for people who came from a SWOMEN background, but that still cannot be compared at the same level as (for instance) a province-wide quota on out-of-province applicants.

What is a person supposed to do if they don't have relatives living in a province who can help them become an IP applicant? What happens if your grades are good, not stellar, but you have the misfortune of being an Ontario resident? What if you didn't marry a spouse who could help you become an IP applicant in Newfoundland?

I only learned of the profound unfairness of the system after multiple failed attempts at application to Ontario medical schools, and applying as an OOP candidate to schools outside of Ontario. I was angry at the system, and I thought that there has to be another way to even out the unfair playing field. This led me on a journey of discovery.

I believed that acceptance to medical school in Canada should not be this difficult. At its core, our system is profoundly unfair. Despite my personal challenges in matriculating at a Canadian school, I refused to pick another career path. I refused to take "no" for an answer and give up on my dream of pursuing medicine. I decided to search for **another option** that would allow me to become a fully licensed doctor in the Canadian healthcare system.

I once met a man who said that, "**the easiest path to becoming a Canadian doctor lies not in Canada**". He was right. I became a licensed doctor in the Canadian healthcare system by going to medical school in the United States.

This was how my personal journey of growth and experience began, out of necessity and recognizing a flawed system for what it is. Whether one becomes a practising MD or practising DO, it really doesn't matter. All I wanted was to be a physician who can help people and to alleviate suffering. There have been many books published on international medical education, and more still on the allopathic MD schools in Canada and the US. What is found lacking is the complete silence of published literature for American osteopathic medical schools, and what Canadians need to know before they make the decision and after they have made the decision. With that in mind, this book will focus on the DO degree, since I come from this background.

References:

(1)https://www.ouac.on.ca/guide/omsas-program-requirements/#totals

Accessed January 20th, 2017.

(2)The University of British Columbia. Faculty of Medicine. MD Undergraduate Program. Frequently asked questions page. Available at:

http://mdprogram.med.ubc.ca/admissions/frequently-asked-questions/
http://mdprogram.med.ubc.ca/files/2016/09/MED-2020-Admissions-Statistics-Website-Final.pdf
(3)http://mdprogram.med.ubc.ca/admissions/admission-requirements/
(4)Memorial University. Faculty of Medicine. Application Evaluation and Competitions page. Available at:
http://www.med.mun.ca/Admissions/ApplicationEvaluationCompetitions.aspx
(5)http://umanitoba.ca/faculties/health_sciences/medicine/admissions/8831.html

The Road Not Taken
Two roads diverged in a yellow wood,
And sorry I could not travel both...

I shall be telling this with a sigh
Somewhere ages and ages hence:
Two roads diverged in a wood, and I,
I took the one less travelled by,
And that has made all the difference.
- Robert Frost

Section 2: My Story

I wasn't always the best student. I got my fair share of Bs and Cs in middle school, and the first two years of high school. Everything changed when my father took me on a vacation to China during the summer break of grade 10 in 2002. I was enthralled by the energy and hunger for power and wealth of an ancient revitalizing civilization. Everywhere I went, there was construction. Skyscrapers were being built everywhere, and there was a sense of revival. I saw my cousins study during their summer vacation. Books upon books of homework to be completed even during the summer break. I saw high school students taking extracurricular classes on Saturdays and Sundays so they could get ahead of their peers. To me, it felt clear. To compete in the 21st century, I had to work a lot harder than I did before.

I completed my last two years of high school with a 92% average. I was among the top of my class. I was accepted into the University of Toronto, Faculty of Arts and Sciences. I was a straight A student throughout my undergraduate studies. My lowest mark in undergrad was an A-, or 80%, or a 3.70. I managed to graduate with a 3.87 cGPA on the American AMCAS scale, or a 3.82 with Ontario OMSAS scale. My cGPA was fairly competitive for medical school application during that time. However, my MCAT wasn't the greatest. I took the MCAT three times, the last score being the highest at 29T (506), with 12 (130) in biological sciences, 10 (127) in physical sciences, 7 (123) in verbal reasoning, and T for the writing section (no longer present on the new MCAT). The MCAT that I took was of course the older version, and the updated version is quite different in content and scoring.

With the old MCAT, a 7 (123) in verbal reasoning was considered fairly low, and below the cut-offs for most of the Ontario medical schools. As a result, I was automatically screened out of those Ontario medical schools with a verbal reasoning cut-off. For the remaining Ontario schools who only looked at the cGPA, my cGPA of 3.82 on the OMSAS scale also happened to be just below their cut-offs as well. So even though I was a straight A student, with my stats of 3.82 cGPA and 29T (506) MCAT, I was denied an interview for all Ontario schools.

I knew that being a doctor was my dream, but owing to my subpar MCAT score, my options were fairly limited. I had a few options at my disposal:

1) Rewrite the MCAT for the 4th time.

2) Do a second undergrad and hope to boost the GPA even more. Or lastly,

3) Look into international medical education such as Ireland, Australia, the Caribbean.

I thought about the predicament I was in for two weeks, and came to the following conclusion: rewriting the MCAT for the fourth time was not an option for me as I simply refused to take that test for a fourth time. Doing a second undergrad in hopes of boosting my GPA was also not an option, as it would take too long to make a significant difference in my GPA, and I didn't want to spend any more years in undergrad. The last option made the most sense to me as it would take me down a path that I was aiming for - that of medicine. I started looking into international medical education, and I started reading every piece of information and anecdotes that I could get my hands on. I was ready to apply to the Caribbean, and I almost became a student at SABA or SGU.

However, the more I looked into international medical education, the more I learned of its dangers. It was not all rainbow and roses like these international schools made it out to be. I started reading about the predictions of the impending shortage of residency spots in the US. How there would be enough residency spots for American medical graduates, and not enough spots for IMGs. I started reading and looking at the abysmal residency match rates for IMGs who managed to make it back for residency training in Canada. I started reading and hearing about horror stories of

Canadians who went to the Caribbean and who ended up not matching, and now owe more than three hundred thousand dollars in debt. I started hearing stories of Caribbean MD grads who went unmatched, and then decided to enrol in school again to become physician assistants in order to find a job and pay off their debt.

It quickly became clear to me that from the 1980s to the early 2000s, the Caribbean and overseas medical education might have been a fair option to pursue medicine, especially if one planned on matching in the US. A fair number of people were making it back to the US and to a lesser degree, Canada. However, the times have changed. One can easily look at recent match results for IMGs in the US and Canada and find all kinds of anecdotes and horror stories of those going unmatched. I came to the conclusion that the days where foreign international medical graduates could ***easily*** match into the US or Canada were long gone.

I realized that international medical education could still work for US citizens, but it was never really designed for Canadians and non-US citizens. US citizens, even if they were international graduates, could interview and match back home into US programs for the simple reason that they are American citizens, and do not need visa sponsorship. This is not the case for Canadians. I realized that a lot of these offshore medical schools, be it Caribbean, Australian, Irish, it didn't matter, made a lot of money off the desperation of Canadians who wanted to pursue a career in medicine.

This was the general situation I was in while applying to medical school. **This continues to be the situation in 2017.** At the time, I was very disheartened. I knew with my stats, I had to improve my MCAT, and try for many more cycles before I had a shot at an interview, let alone matriculate at a Canadian medical school. What had seemed to be a sure route - that of international medical education, turned out to also be filled with hardship and uncertainty. Surely, there must be another option where I can pursue my dreams of becoming a physician?

Then I remembered, I had read something online about "**DOs**", or "**osteopathic physicians**" in the US. Could this be the last option I was searching for? I started to research the DO route in earnest, I started reading every piece of literature I could find, I looked at DO match data in the US, I looked at the provinces where USDOs (at the time) could match in the first iteration with CMGs in Canada, I looked at the licensing exams and requirements for DOs, I looked into OMM or osteopathic manipulative medicine. I learned that the curriculum for both MD and DO schools were basically the same, with the DO schools adding another approximately two hundred hours of hands on OMM education to their pre-clinical science curriculum. The whole enterprise took me two weeks, by which time I was satisfied with the information I had obtained.

My research resonated with the kind of physician that I aspired to be. Specifically, I wished to pursue a career in primary health care. Osteopathic medicine also has a strong emphasis on primary care. I want to pursue primary care because there is heavy emphasis on the interaction with patients, treatment of undifferentiated problems, and disease prevention – all these things I consider to be the hallmarks of a good doctor.

I wanted to pursue osteopathic medicine because from an educational point of view, I thought that I would learn ***more*** medicine in an osteopathic program than an allopathic one. All topics of modern medicine are covered by both MD and DO programs, but DOs learn the something more, this being **osteopathic manipulative medicine**. After two weeks of research on the DO route, this was my mindset.

At the time of my application in 2008, most people in Canada did not have a good idea of what a US trained DO was. Most people were ignorant of the fact that they were considered equal in practice rights to MDs. A career as an osteopathic physician in Canada was the epitome of the road less travelled. I was sold! I decided to pursue the DO degree as a route to medicine.

I ended up applying to American DO schools in mid November of 2008, which was very late in the cycle. I had problems with the MCAT prometrics center. I was initially supposed to write the MCAT in mid June, but after a series of setbacks with prometric's computer system, my results came out in mid-late October 2008. By that time, the deadline for most US MD schools was passed, and I never really properly applied to US MD schools as a result. Fortunate for me, mid-late November happened to be right at the end of the application cycle for US DO schools; I ended up interviewing at two DO schools, and was waitlisted with a guaranteed seat for the DO class of 2014 in my first choice - Western University of Health Sciences - College of Osteopathic Medicine of the Pacific.

Section 3:
Do your own research, make your own conclusions, and beware of laypersons

Parents unfortunately fall under this category and can be one of the main barriers to the correct choice of medical institution. By this, I mean that the vast majority of parents are not well informed (why would they be?), yet still have a strong say in which route their children take. This is especially the case where parents are the ones who will be paying the tuition.

If you are a parent to a pre-med and you are reading this book, please understand that a MD degree can be obtained almost ***anywhere***. It is where and ***if*** you match into a residency program that truly matters.

I have seen cases where parents are extremely adamant about their children attending a school that gives the "MD" degree, regardless of whether these schools are located in the Caribbean or other developing countries. The misconception runs deep, and these parents seem to think that getting a "MD" is a sure ticket to a good life for their children. They could not be more mistaken, and more misinformed about the current reality of medical education.

This is especially true for people of South Asian heritage. I have seen many instances where the parents have a strong say in where the pre-med ends up after a few failed application cycles in Canada or the US. At one point, I came across an Indian man who was bragging to his co-workers that his daughter is going to be a doctor, and is attending medical school. When asked where she goes for medical school, he answered "Romania", completely unaware of the stigma of being an IMG, and the uphill battle his daughter has to face when trying to match into a residency program in the US or Canada as an IMG.

I have seen quite a few examples where the pre-med was set on going to a US based DO school. They applied, interviewed and was accepted, yet they were strongly discouraged by their parents and went to an international school instead, despite all the issues that come with an IMG background in Canada, and to a lesser extent in the US.

Part of the problem lies with the general lack of knowledge that pre-med undergrads have regarding medical education, and graduate medical education. At the time of graduation from undergrad, the average pre-med's knowledge of the processes required to become a fully licensed physician is somewhere along the line of:

1) Matriculate into a med school,
2) Graduate from med school,
3) Match into a residency program,
4) Success! Financial future is secured perpetually.

This is about the extent of their knowledge.

Unfortunately, this whole process really is an art form, and the path is laden with traps along the way. It is vital to have as clear a roadmap as possible to avoid any and all pitfalls during this journey.

This book aspires to be the exact guide that so many pre-meds did not have before. Hence the name of the book, "The Canadian Guide".

"The bravest are surely those who have the clearest vision of what is before them, glory and danger alike, and yet notwithstanding, go out to meet it."

- Thucydides

Part One

What you need to know as a pre-med

Section 4:
Basics of American medical education

What is osteopathic medicine?

Some say that osteopathic medicine is the best kept secret in medicine!

In the United States, there are two types of complete physicians - DOs (Doctor of Osteopathic Medicine) and MDs (Doctor of Allopathic Medicine). Both physicians are trained in the full spectrum of clinical and medical sciences and are allowed to practice in any specialty, prescribe any medication, and perform surgery (1). More important, DOs and MDs share equal rights (1, 2). In addition to the basic medical science curriculum present in both MD and DO schools, DOs complete an additional (over) one hundred hours of training in **osteopathic manipulative therapy (OMT)** - a hands-on approach to treat the body's musculoskeletal system (1, 2).

Osteopathic physicians train with a greater holistic approach and tactile appreciation of the anatomy of the human body relative to their allopathic counterparts. Osteopathic physicians have traditionally served as **primary care physicians** in the United States. Osteopathic students are required to take and pass a national board examination, known as the **Comprehensive Osteopathic Medicine Licensing Examination (COMLEX)**. Allopathic graduates are required to take and pass the **United States Medical Licensing Examination (USMLE)**. It is not uncommon for osteopathic students to take both the COMLEX and the USMLE when applying for postgraduate training.

Upon successful completion of medical school and postgraduate training, DOs are granted full medical practice rights in the US and in all provinces of Canada.

Osteopathic physicians have the additional benefit of entering postgraduate training programs with either the **American Osteopathic Association (AOA)** or the **Accreditation Council for Graduate Medical Education (ACGME)**.

To date, there are currently 70,000 MDs in Canada. In the US alone, there are over 63,000 active osteopathic physicians in practice (3).

Reference:

(1) Shannon SC, Teitelbaum HS. The status and future of osteopathic medical education in the United States. Acad Med. 2009 Jun; 84 (6):707-11.
(2) Gevitz N. The transformation of osteopathic medical education. Acad Med. 2009 Jun; 84 (6):701-6.
(3) Young A, Chaudhry HJ, Rhyne J. Dugan M. A Census of Actively Licensed Physicians in the United States, 2010. Journal of Medical Regulation 2010 96(4); 11-20.

Strength of American osteopathic medical education:

For the 2016-2017 cycle, the **American Association of Colleges of Osteopathic Medicine (AACOM)** received 185,602 individual school applications from 20,720 applicants (1), with a total of 7,369 new students starting their medical education at one of the 33 DO-granting medical schools at 44 locations in 31 states (2).

Today, more than twenty percent of U.S. medical students are training at osteopathic medical schools (3).

Reference:

(1) http://www.aacom.org/docs/default-source/data-and-trends/2016-aacomas-applicant-pool-profile-summary-report.pdf?sfvrsn=12
Accessed Jan 23rd, 2017.

(2) https://www.aacom.org/news-and-events/publications/iome/by-topic/research/2016/10/20/fall-2016-preliminary-enrollment
Accessed Jan 23rd, 2017.

(3) http://www.aacom.org/become-a-doctor/about-om
Accessed Jan 23rd, 2017

Canadian enrolment in American osteopathic medical schools:

When I was started attending a DO medical school in 2010, there were 84 applicants and only 10 Canadians who matriculated at DO schools across the US.

For the 2016 entering class, we now have 263 applicants and 64 Canadians matriculating at US DO schools. 2015 and 2016 saw our largest number of applicants at 263 (1).

	2009	2010	2011	2012	2013	2014	2015	2016
Number of Canadian DO Applicants	66	84	114	145	175	210	263	263
Number of Canadian DO Matriculates	13	10	40	37	58	56	67	64

Figure 1. Canadian applicants and matriculants to American osteopathic medical schools per annum

As you can see from these numbers, there has been an almost a sixfold increase in the number of Canadian matriculants since 2010.

In comparison, the Northern Ontario School of Medicine (NOSM) (Sudbury, Ontario) has a class size of approximately 60 a year. There is essentially a NOSM sized DO-granting school training Canadians in the US right now. Like it or lot, these numbers of US trained Canadian DOs will have ramifications for the Canadian health care system in the coming years.

Canadians are now becoming so well known in American osteopathic medical schools that **Johns Hopkins University** even mentioned the COA, MSU's Canadian initiative, and COMSA on their website! (2)

References:

(1) American Association of Colleges of Osteopathic Medicine (AACOM). Applicants and matriculants. Chevy Chase, MD: 2017. Available at:

http://www.aacom.org/data/applicantsmatriculants/Pages/default.aspx
(2)http://studentaffairs.jhu.edu/preprofadvising/pre-medhealth/applicants/special-applicant-groups/canadian-applicants/
Accessed December 20th, 2014.

What makes a DO different from a MD?

DOs and MDs have the same exact practice rights, take the same classes. The difference comes in that DOs are taught an additional skill - **osteopathic manipulative medicine (OMM)**, which stems from the idea that structure and function of the body are interrelated. Based on this theory, any misalignment of the spine or joints causing impingement on nerves or fascia can cause the body to function less than optimally.

Osteopathic manipulation is gentle, directed manipulation of the spine, limbs, and joints that aims to restore the body to its optimal structure so it can resume optimal function. OMM is applicable for a wide variety of other complaints. If you are interested in applying to a DO school, you should be familiar with OMM and the theory behind it, and be able to explain why it appeals to you.

What is the difference between an osteopath and an osteopathic physician?

Only in the United States are holders of the DO degree considered "medical doctors" equivalent to practice rights as MDs. There are also osteopathic colleges in Canada, England, Europe and beyond. For example, there is the Canadian College of Osteopathy (http://www.osteopathy-canada.com/) who also gives the "DO" degree. But graduates from these DO "colleges" are only limited to osteopathic manipulation (which is the cornerstone that makes osteopathic medicine different from allopathic medicine). These guys did not receive the **full medical training that American DOs receive**. These "osteopaths", not "osteopathic doctors", are not medical doctors, cannot register with the CPSO, or any medical specialty in Canada or the US. Osteopaths are not osteopathic doctors, and they are in the same category as naturopaths, chiropractors. US trained DOs (osteopathic physicians) on the other hand are full medical doctors.

Andrew Taylor Still is the founder of osteopathic medicine in the US. He had many students, not all of which were Americans. Some of his American students left the US, moved to other countries (e.g., Canada, England, Scandinavia, and beyond), and took osteopathic medicine with them.

Nearly one hundred years ago, the American DO doctors of that era are like the DO "osteopaths" you see in Canada and other countries today. They were not recognized as "doctors". After decades of development within the osteopathic profession in the US, they eventually began to incorporate the four years of medical education (the MD part) into the DO curriculum. Add a few more decades of advocacy work for equality between the MD and DO worlds, USDOs eventually gained "doctor" status in all fifty states equivalent to that of the MDs.

Unfortunately, this slow process of transformation from a fringe group of "osteopaths" to a mainstream provider of healthcare (osteopathic medicine) in the US did not replicate in other parts of the world. The students of Andrew Taylor Still who left the US held onto the core elements of osteopathy - the OMM part, but never added the MD curriculum into their teachings. As such, only DOs trained in US medical schools are recognized as doctors, and not graduates of DO "colleges" outside of the US. Also as a twist of history, these DO osteopaths are also legally known as "DOs", and can call themselves "osteopaths", but they cannot call themselves "doctors".

Now, fast forward to the present time, DO osteopaths co-exist in Canada along with US trained DOs. DO osteopaths, sometimes called **DO(q)**, provide OMM treatment, and has survived in Canada for nearly a hundred years. If an osteopath DO starts to call himself an osteopathic doctor and starts prescribing medication, then the **Canadian Osteopathic Association (COA)** and the provincial licensing authorities are obliged to pursue them for practicing without a license.

List of important websites to continue your research:
American Osteopathic Association (AOA)
www.osteopathic.org
Canadian Osteopathic Association (COA)
www.osteopathic.ca
Canadian Osteopathic Medical Student Association (COMSA)
www.studentdo.ca

Section 5:
Basics of American osteopathic medical school admissions

Canadian prerequisites, transcripts and foreign evaluations:

Canadian prerequisites are acceptable. However, there is a distinction between Quebec and the rest of Canada that becomes relevant when you are submitting your transcripts.

Transcripts that are in French are considered "foreign coursework", and French transcripts would need to go through a **foreign evaluation service** (1). This would be the case for those universities in Quebec that are French only.

Transcripts that are in English however are not considered foreign, and would not need to go through an assessment.

References:

(1)http://help.unicas.com:8888/aacomasHelpPages/instructions/how-to-send-transcripts/foreign-and-french-canadian-transcripts/index.html
Accessed February 3rd, 2017.

What is a credit hour/semester hour and what is the Canadian equivalent?

For AACOM (or AAMC) application purposes, full credit courses (1.0 credit) with labs are considered to have 8 semester hours. Full credit (1.0 credit) courses without lab are considered to have 6 hours. Half credit courses (0.5 credit) with lab are considered to have 4 credits, while half credit (0.5 credit) courses without lab are considered to have 3 credits. Basically, what this means is that Canadian schools do not give you 2 extra semester hours for labs in the courses. And yes, half credit courses (with OR without lab) are only "worth" 3 semester hours, while full credit courses (with or without lab) are only "worth" 6 hours. BUT the AACOM knows this Canadian difference, so they will adjust accordingly (and if not, your school will know of this difference so your school admission will adjust accordingly). On you AACOM application, you should write down the full name of the course followed by whether this course has a lab or not (e.g. BIO150Y1Y - Organisms in their environment (with lab)), vs. (ANT203Y1Y - Human Evolution (no lab)). The vast majority of problems can be avoided by doing this.

What are competitive cGPA and MCAT scores for matriculants?

In 2015, the average MCAT for matriculants was 27.33 (1) and the average cGPA was 3.53 (1).

Unfortunately, there is currently no information on the average scores via the new MCAT.

As the number of applicants increase each year, the average MCAT score will continue to creep up. While you can expect to get interviewed at many schools with a score in the mid to high 20s (499 - 507 via the new MCAT), the average of some of the more competitive schools are approaching 30 and above (508+). One should obtain a MCAT score in the high 20s to low 30s (507 - 508) to be considered fairly competitive for DO medical schools.

A 3.50 cGPA and above would be considered fairly competitive. DO medical schools are known to look at the "whole application", and is not as picky as the MD schools regarding the hard stats. A high cGPA can offset a lower MCAT, and a higher MCAT can offset a lower cGPA. Life experiences in the form of previous careers can also offset lower MCAT and cGPA scores.

References:

(1)http://www.aacom.org/become-a-doctor/applying/general-admission-requirements Accessed February 3rd, 2017.

Do you need a D.O. reference letter?

You do not necessarily need a D.O. reference letter for medical school application. Many schools will accept a MD letter in place of a DO letter. Furthermore, it is often very difficult to find a DO in Canada.

However, it is to your advantage to get a D.O. letter even if that means going over the border to obtain one. Remember you have little time and it is imperative to have your application completed as early as possible.

If you want to find a DO to shadow **within** Canada, your best option is to contact the **Canadian**

Osteopathic Medical Student Association (COMSA) (http://www.studentdo.ca), and ask if they have DO physicians near the city you reside in.

Experiential pearl:

I didn't do any shadowing, DO or MD. I obtained a letter from a MD/PhD that I was doing research with. I was able to fulfil that letter requirement with my MD letter, and I didn't bother applying to schools that only wanted a DO letter due to time constraint.

How should I prepare for the interview?

It used to be the case that American medical school interviews tend to have a very relaxed atmosphere, and the candidate is asked a series of questions either with one or more interviewers. In this context, all the candidate had to do to prepare was to research and gain a fair understanding of how the American health care system works, and to be able to answer questions about themselves, and what makes medicine the right path for them. It is to be expected that interviews at US DO schools will involve at least one or more questions regarding the DO philosophy, and why one would choose to come to a DO school, as opposed to a MD school. One must then prepare to have a good understanding of the DO philosophy, and its differences to allopathic medicine. **"The DO"** is a good book regarding osteopathic medicine in the US, and some have found it extremely useful for their interview preparation.

In general, there are many books available that talks about preparation for medical school interviews, with sample answers supplied by previously successful matriculants to medical school. It could prove beneficial to obtain one or more of these books and to read them to gain a good comprehension of the questions that are asked, and answers to respond to them.

More recently, American medical schools have transitioned to **MMI - multiple mini interviews** as the format to select candidates. This is fairly new, and it was not very prevalent when I interviewed for medical school years ago. There are also many books on the market dealing with MMI format. There are even preparation courses that offer practical training, mock MMIs as a way to help you prepare for this format. I would encourage you to obtain these books and look into these commercial courses as a way to prepare for the MMI format.

Experiential pearl:

On **studentdoctor.net (SDN)**, there are databases of interview questions from each of the US medical schools (MD or DO) that candidates have been asked in the past. These questions were then recorded on SDN and any user can quite easily access this database.

I made a forty page word document with almost every possible question that was asked over the past 10 years (for my first choice school). Then I memorized to great clarity the answers I had for each potential question. I rehearsed my answers in my mind over and over again, and sometimes I would sit in front of a mirror when I rehearsed my answers. I felt like an actor, memorizing my lines, and acting out my facial expressions and hand movements when I was asked these questions. When interview day came, I was well prepared, and I had anticipated most if not all the answers that the interviewers had in store for me.

Are there any tips that you could give out to Canadians who are taking this path?

1) The first thing to do is find a GPA conversion scale. Convert all your undergraduate grades into a cumulative GPA with the AMCAS scale. A lot of people come to me and give me their average, in numbers. An 80% average is not very helpful to determine your competitiveness if you cannot convert that number into a cGPA on a 4.0 AMCAS scale.

2) Apply as soon as possible. As soon as the AACOM website application comes out in early May of each year, you should begin the process and submit your application as fast as you can. American medical schools (both MD and DO) use "**rolling admission**". What this means is that applicants are accepted throughout the year, so they don't have a system like Canada where the applicant would get their acceptance or rejection all on the same day via mass mail/email. In the US system, for both MD and DO schools, this would mean that applicants are at a great advantage if they apply ahead of the rest of the pack. Specifically, apply as soon as possible.

3) Pick and choose which schools to apply to rigorously. If schools only want a DO letter, chances are, you won't be able to get one unless you are willing to head down to the US for a couple weeks specifically to find a DO to shadow. Most DO schools that require DO letters will also alternatively take a MD letter.

4) Speed is of the essence. If you do manage to secure an interview, and it is mid February - mid March, I would strongly encourage you to overnight any documents pertinent to acceptances - the last thing you want is to wait an entire year on the accepted wait list.

5) I wish I had spent more time with family, friends, went out more, and maintained relationships. You see, to a certain degree, DO programs are not hard pressed for extremely high stats. If you happened to have a lower cGPA, or lower MCAT scores, it will not make or break your application. You don't have to have very high stats to be accepted, although it would certainly help with acceptance. When the average cGPA for for the accepted matriculants to some schools hover around 3.4 to 3.6, I felt like my cGPA of 3.87 was overkill, and I could have spent some of the time I did in school to improve other aspects of my life.

A word about the University of Toronto (UofT):

The University of Toronto truly is a great and world class institution. I graduated from this place for my undergraduate studies and I have experienced its rigorous curriculum. Having come from this background, I don't think it is the best school to easily attain a high GPA for purposes of medical school application. Of course, there will always be those people who excel in any environment, no matter how difficult. But my experience is that for the average person, it will be extremely difficult to obtain a competitive cGPA.

Also, there are issues with UofT's general chemistry department when one is applying to medical school in the US. You see, in the US, they need **one full credit of general chemistry with lab**. However, at the University of Toronto, only half a credit worth of general chemistry with lab is offered. As such, many UofT graduates eventually realize that their cGPA is below the cut-offs for Canadian medical schools, but they also cannot apply to US medical schools because are missing the half credit of general chemistry prerequisite. They are then forced to go to another institute to fulfil the general chemistry requirement.

Clinical pearl:

This exact situation happened to me. When I was applying to US med schools, I was missing the general chemistry credit. I had to enrol at the neighbouring University - Ryerson, to fulfil the general chemistry requirements. It took me an 6 extra months to do that.

UofT is a great place for research, but if your end goal is medicine, or any professional school, I would recommend against attending UofT for undergraduate studies.

Help! I went to the University of Toronto (UofT) but they don't have a second half credit of general chemistry with lab!

UofT offers a first year undergraduate half credit inorganic chemistry course (formerly known as CHM139H1) with lab, but there's no subsequent follow up course for inorganic chemistry (i.e. general chemistry) that includes a lab (making up a full credit). Most people take CHM220H1, an analytic chemistry course, but that course does not include a lab component, and it is quite difficult.

It has been many years since I attended UofT for my undergraduate studies, during this time, they may or may not have remedied this issue of not offering a second half credit of inorganic chemistry with lab. What I would recommend when any prerequisite credit courses is missing for one's US medical school application while attending UofT is to take continuing education courses at **Chang School of Continuing**

Education at **Ryerson University** - which happens to be a few city blocks away from the downtown University of Toronto campus.

Experiential pearl:

What I did to remedy the problem was I redid my general chemistry course work at Ryerson University (walking distance from UofT). I've had very good experience with Ryerson. I took their **continuing education** courses at night. Specifically, I took a half credit general chemistry lecture course - **CCHY 103 General Chemistry I**, followed by a half credit general chemistry lab course - **CKCH 107 General Chemistry Laboratory**. These two courses combined to give one full credit of general chemistry, and they were acceptable to all the US medical schools that I had applied to.

I strongly urge you to visit the website of the **Chang School of Continuing Education** of Ryerson University (http://ce-online.ryerson.ca/ce/) to find the current chemistry courses offered.

In terms of difficulty, the courses at the **Chang School** were significantly easier than anything I have taken at UofT. I will also add that while I was there, many UofT students were also there taking these two courses to fulfil their general chemistry credit requirement for US medical/dental/pharmacy schools. It was really quite a sight to behold. A good fraction of those two chemistry classes at Ryerson were housed by UofT students.

However, I can not guarantee if the MD/DO medical school in the US that you are applying to will accept these courses. I made sure these two courses were acceptable before taking them. So likewise, I would strongly recommend that you get in contact with the admissions office of the MD/DO schools you applied to, and then confirm that the prerequisite courses you are taking will be acceptable.

"Sokath! His eyes open!"

Section 6: American medical education compared to international options

What kind of attitude should I take if I am considering international options?

With all of the "out of Canada" medical school options, regardless if it is a Caribbean MD, an Irish or Australian MBBS, one needs to be comfortable with the fact that **they might never end up coming back to practice in Canada**. The moment you go outside Canada for medical school, you should be comfortable with the fact that you might be forced to match and practice in the United States for a long period of time. This is simple reality and the faster one accepts this fact, the better the situation for all involved. The worst possible attitude a pre-med might have when choosing a Caribbean MD or an Irish or Australian MBBS school is to expect to easily make it back into Canada for residency. The chances are truly stacked against you, and it is often not feasible to make it back to Canada for residency.

Why should I choose an American DO or MD medical school over an international school?

The MD and DO degrees are both bona fide North American medical degrees. The DO and MD degrees are considered equivalent by the medical jurisdictions in both the US and Canada. Just like the MD degree, the DO medical degree will give the wielder full practice rights in all of the US and Canada.

During the NRMP match for ACGME accredited residency programs, graduates of American osteopathic and allopathic medical schools (i.e. AMGs) perform much better and have a much higher chance at a successful match. Again, **the important part of medical education is not so much where you go to school, or the name of your medical degree, but whether you can match into your preferred residency program for post graduate training.**

The reason you should choose an American DO or MD medical school over an international medical school is because as an AMG, you will be **virtually guaranteed a US residency position**. The same cannot be said for non-US citizens of international medical schools.

The ease with which Canadian AMGs can obtain an ACGME residency spot is simple indisputable reality. This being the case, as Canadians, it does not make sense to go overseas to a foreign medical school, be it a Caribbean MD or European MBBS, to become a CSA, then an IMG and be forced to deal with all the issues facing IMGs, such as the abysmal match rate, inferior visas, and a real possibility of being in serious debt and not securing a residency.

This is a simple issue of graduating as an American medical graduate, where you have the full benefits of going to a US accredited medical school, compared to the difficult path of going through the IMG route and facing a much lower residency match rate. If you still insist on going to an international medical school, make sure you know what you are getting yourself into.

Let us take a look at data published by CaRMS to drive this point home. **In the 2016 CaRMS match, only 408 of the 1815 (22.5%) IMGs or Canadians studying abroad managed to secure a residency in Canada** (1). **Even for US MDs, only 18 out of 33 (54.5%) were able to successfully match into a Canadian residency program** (1).

The US has historically been the country that was most friendly to international medical graduates. IMGs have made up large portions of the American medical system in the past, and they continue to do so. Every year, tens of thousands of IMGs apply to US ACGME residency programs, and thousands are successful in securing a residency spot. **The success rate for an IMG to match into an US ACGME residency program is much higher than that of Canada - in 2016, the match rate was 50.5% versus the Canadian 22.5%** (1, 2), more than double.

Figure 2. CaRMS and NRMP match data from 2013 to 2016 (1, 2).

With the unpredictability of the Canadian match, ensuring success when attending an "out of Canada" medical school would mean to maximize your chances with the NRMP match for ACGME programs.

Figure 2 shows the compiled CaRMS data for IMGs and AMGs, as well as NRMP data for IMGs without US citizenship between the years 2013 to 2016. One can see that with a non-US IMG background, there is a much

	2013	2014	2015	2016
IMG CaRMS	499/2216 (22.5%)	449/2318 (19.4%)	421/1984 (21.2%)	408/1815 (22.5%)
AMG CaRMS	25/47 (53.2%)	27/41 (65.8%)	26/44 (59.1%)	18/33 (54.5%)
Non-US IMG NRMP	3,556/7,568 (47.0%)	3,633/ 7,334 (49.5%)	3,641/7,366 (49.4%)	3,769/7,460 (50.5%)

higher chance of a successful match through the NRMP.

Reference:

(1) Canadian Resident Matching Service (CaRMS). Reports & Statistics - R-1 Match Reports - 2016. Ottawa, ON: Canadian Resident Matching Service; 2016. Available at:
http://www.CaRMS.ca/en/data-and-reports/r-1/

(2) National Residency Matching Program- Results and Data, 2016 Main Residency Match. Washington DC. 2016 Available at:
http://www.nrmp.org/wp-content/uploads/2016/04/Main-Match-Results-and-Data-2016.pdf

The success of USDOs versus IMGs in the NRMP match

Enrolment into Canadian medical schools has become increasingly difficult and has forced many students to seek medical education abroad (1). However, the increase in international medical enrolment has exceeded the number of postgraduate training opportunities in Canada (2). Consequently, **many Canadian graduates of international schools are forced to secure residency programs in the United States but have had very limited success**. Of the 7,460 active non-US citizen IMG applicants for ACGME postgraduate training in 2016, only 3,769 (50.5%) succeeded at securing a residency position (3). As a result, IMGs including Canadian graduates are burdened with extensive school debt and lack practice privileges.

When compared to DOs participating in the 2016 match, 2,396 of the 2,982 students (80.3%) were able to secure an ACGME accredited residency position (Figure 3) (3). The ability to secure proper ACGME accredited post-graduate training in the United States continues to make osteopathic medicine highly attractive to Canadian students versus traditional IMG programs.

	Active non-US citizen IMG applicants	Active osteopathic applicants	Active allopathic applicants	Active Canadian applicants
2013	3,556 / 7,568 (47.0%)	2,002 / 2,677 (74.8%)	16,390 / 17,487 (93.7%)	14 / 21 (66.6%)
2014	3,633/ 7,334 (49.5%)	2,127 / 2,738 (77.7%)	16,399 / 17,374 (94.4%)	6 / 14 (42.9%)
2015	3,641 / 7,366 (49.4%)	2,339 / 2,949 (79.3%)	16,932 / 18,025 (93.9%)	17 / 24 (70.8%)

2016	3,769 / 7,460 (50.5%)	2,396 / 2,982 (80.3%)	17,057 / 18,187 (93.8%)	13 / 15 (86.6%)

Figure 3. American match statistics for ACGME post-graduate training 2013 - 2016.

Graduates of American DO and MD medical schools have much higher match rates compared to IMGs. Figure 3 illustrates the match rates of American MD graduates, DO graduates, Canadian MD graduates, and non-US citizen IMGs who participated in the NRMP match from 2013 - 2016. As you can see from the data, American DO graduates have an almost **30% higher chance** at the NRMP match than non-US citizen IMGs!

The numbers do not lie, it is a much riskier proposition to match as an IMG than a American DO or MD graduate through the NRMP.

References:

(1) Watts E, Davies JC, Metcalfe D. The Canadian International Medical Graduate
Bottleneck: A New Problem for New Doctors. Canadian Medical Education Journal 2011; 2(2): 86-90.

(2) Canadian Resident Matching Service (CaRMS). Reports & Statistics - R-1 Match Reports - 2016. Ottawa, ON: Canadian Resident Matching Service; 2016. Available at:
http://www.CaRMS.ca/en/data-and-reports/r-1/reports-2016/

(3) National Residency Matching Program- Results and Data, 2016 Main Residency Match. Washington DC. 2016 Available at:

http://www.nrmp.org/wp-content/uploads/2016/04/Main-Match-Results-and-Data-2016.pdf

How do I maximize my chance at a successful residency match?

The simplest way to practice medicine in Canada is to graduate from a Canadian medical school. But due to the fierce and competitive nature of Canadian medical school entrance, this is not an easy or realistic goal for many Canadians.

One can bypass the roadblock of Canadian medical school entrance by going abroad for medical school, either in the United States or at an international institution. One can then hope to match back home to Canada for residency. However, the Canadian residency match is difficult for non-Canadian graduates, even if one was an AMG, the chance of matching into a Canadian program is limited.

If a Canadian ends up going to medical school outside of Canada, then it is in their best interest to **match into an ACGME program in the United States** through the NRMP. In order to maximize their chance with the NRMP match, it is in their best interest to first **be an AMG by virtue of going to a American medical school**, be it a MD- or DO-granting institution.

In short, for Canadians who go outside of Canada for medical school, the best strategy to maximize their chance at a successful residency match is to **attend an American medical school, and then to match into an American ACGME program**.

Why do hundreds of Canadians still go to international medical schools each year?

There are a numerous reasons for why this is still the case.

1) Many pre-meds who consider going to international medical schools are very uninformed of the risks they are taking when they leave Canada. They did not do their due diligence and research these things thoroughly. Many of them are **not even aware that the osteopathic medical degree exists**!

On several occasions, I have met IMGs or received emails from IMGs who tell me that they wish they had known about the US DO option before starting at a foreign medical school, for the simple reason that they did not know of the very existence of the US DO degree.

2). There is a chronic issue of poor visibility of Canadian DO physicians due to our historically low numbers (a situation that is beginning to reverse slowly). Due to our low numbers, we have **poor brand recognition in Canada**. Even in 2017, there are less than thirty US trained DOs practicing in all of Canada.

3) There is also a **lack of marketing by DO schools**. US DO schools never seek out Canadians, but Irish, Australian and Caribbean schools spent significant effort and money marketing their brand in Canada.

In large Canadian cities, one can easily see Caribbean medical school advertisements on the subway system. These advertisements paint a rosy picture of Caribbean schools, basically stating that you do not require high stats, nor in some cases need the MCAT to enrol in these places. Unfortunately for the Canadian consumer, these advertisements do not at all mention the abysmal IMG match rates in the US and Canada that awaits them four years down the road.

The reason you don't see any US MD or DO marketing to Canadian applicants is that American medical schools do not have a shortage of applicants, as might be the case for international schools. When I applied to medical school in 2009, the school where I matriculated had 4500 applicants, where 500 interviews were given for 223 spots. The number of applicants that the average American medical school receive easily rival or exceed most Canadian medical schools.

The Irish or Australian gamble

Some Australian and Irish medical schools offer 5-6 year entrance programs tailored to students straight out of high school. If one is successful at matching into a residency right after graduating from such a program, then this would be a very attractive option. The benefit is that one can potentially avoid spending 4-5 years of time doing an undergraduate degree after high school. You can graduate with a medical degree in your early twenties as a result. **If** you then manage to match into residency (either US or Canada), **then** you would have won the Irish or Australian gamble.

Why did you win? You won because you managed to save 4-5 years of time by bypassing undergrad, and you will be the youngest person in your residency program as a result of this gamble. This strategy fits well with my general strategy of getting to where you want in the shortest amount of time. **The successful application of the "Irish or Australian gamble" is the only circumstance where I would suggest that going to an Irish or Australian medical school is worthwhile.**

Be warned that this is a **gamble**. You may save 4-5 years of time avoiding an undergraduate degree, but

what if you do not match into a residency program in either the US or Canada due to the difficulties facing the route of an IMG? In this sense, it is a gamble. The successful application of this strategy will save you a number of years and make you the youngest resident in your program. The unsuccessful application will also make you an extremely young medical school graduate, but you may end up being a very young unmatched international medical graduate with a large loan you must now repay.

Let me explain. As I will state again and again in this book, if one is an IMG or CSA, then one's game plan should always be to seek an ACGME accredited residency program. However, international schools outside of the Caribbean (e.g. Irish medical schools) rarely dedicate any time on the USMLEs. Their curriculum is not designed to accommodate the USMLEs, and the candidate in these schools must take the time themselves to study for the USMLEs. As such, many people who go to international schools outside the Caribbean (such as Ireland, Australia, schools in Commonwealth countries) often end up not taking the USMLEs. **Not taking the USMLEs is a huge risk**, and is very concerning because the possibility of an IMG or CSA matching back into Canada for residency is still quite low.

The other issue is that you must go to a foreign country right out of high school, when you are 17-18 years old. One may not have the acquired the life skills necessary at that point to be living by themselves, let alone succeed in medical school.

I have met a person who won the Irish Gamble. This individual is one of the youngest people in their residency program; their age is that of someone who would have recently graduated from an undergraduate program. Their future is looking very bright at this point because when you are 22 and starting residency, you are sure to have a sound financial future ahead of you.

Why I chose US DO medical school over the other international options

I have also researched the Caribbean, Irish, Australian options, but the barriers to residency were simply too much for me to accept. I was well on my way to completing my undergraduate degree, so taking the "**Irish or Australian gamble**" was not an option for me. Furthermore, right after high school, I nor my family could afford 100,000 Euros a year for five to six years to attend an Irish medical school. I would say that the costs are too high for most Canadians. I wanted to do my medical school in the US or Canada, and did not wish to go to a different continent.

I read up extensively on online forums and professional organization websites regarding my career prospects as a US DO, versus a MD, versus an IMG. The consensus was that if your stats were slightly on the lower side, and you wished to remain in North America, the best option is to matriculate in an American osteopathic medical school because they look for a "more rounded" applicant and don't focus as much on the strict MCAT or cGPA cut-offs.

I have actually come across several Americans who chose DO medical schools over MD schools. That is to say, they were accepted into MD schools, but they gave it up to attend a DO school. The reasons varied from cost of tuition, to proximity to relatives, to having a tradition of DOs who practice medicine in their family through the generations. I believe that this behaviour speaks volumes to quality and impression that osteopathic medical schools have made on the American public.

From my own assessment after reading about the match rates, the learning experience of IMGs versus DOs, the freedom of movement as an IMG in Canada, my conclusion was that the US DO option was the safer, better and more logical choice compared to all the international options. It became clear to me that as an IMG or CSA, you will have a distinct disadvantage once you start applying for residencies in the US and Canada. However, if you are graduating from a US medical school, you will be considered an AMG. You will then have a much better chance of getting into your desired residency in the US.

Additionally, many international options like some Australian medical schools are taking on more international students than they can handle. There can be as many as 500 people in some Australian first year medical school classes. For certain basic science courses like human anatomy, there can be almost 3 digit numbers of students per cadaver. One truly wonders about the quality of education with such large numbers.

Stories such as not enough internship spots for internationals (i.e., Canadian students) in Australia are also becoming more common. In August 10th, 2010, an article published in **The Sydney Morning Herald** under the title "**Anger over lack of medical internships**" reported that "more than 100 graduates failed to get internships in public hospitals". Another piece published August 16th, 2010 by **ABC Australia** under the title "**Hospitals struggling to meet intern demands**" also reported the inability of public hospitals to provide internship positions for all.

Many international medical schools are cashing in on the boom of Canadians who have gone overseas for medical education over the past few years. All I can say on the subject of going to an international medical school is to do your research very carefully, but go at your own risk.

What is it like to apply for residency as an IMG in Canada or the US?

First hand observation in Canada:

The following is a response by a practicing physician in British Columbia when a comment was made that Canadians at Caribbean medical schools have matched into competitive specialties at the University of Toronto:

"You know of many Canadians (who matched) but I'm sure there are also many who didn't match who you never hear of.

I see the struggles IMGs face (both Canadian-born who went abroad and newer Canadians who immigrated here) and it's not pretty. For Round 2 of CaRMS, my program (which isn't even that competitive to get into in Round 1) got 122 applications for 1 spot. The vast majority were IMGs who went to Ireland, Australia, and the Caribbean who didn't match first round.

Yes, you will hear of the one or two grads who went to SGU and got derm somewhere. But what you won't hear about are the countless others who make it through four-five years of med school, only to get rejected again in trying to secure a residency. Going overseas (non-LCME) is a ***HUGE*** *risk and don't fool yourself into thinking that it's not."*

His quote ought to cement the fact that aiming solely for Canadian residencies while overlooking US ones is a very bad idea.

An IMG is an IMG in Canada; it doesn't matter where one obtained their medical education outside of North America. Someone who went to Oxford England for their medical education will be treated the same as someone who went to Romania for their medical education. The process is extremely difficult, with the odds truly stacked against you.

First hand observation in the US:

The following was a contribution made by a former pre-medical student who was looking into the attitudes that American program directors had regarding American medical education versus international medical education:

"I emailed 40 program directors for 40 different residency programs in CA (the state I want to do residency) and proposed a hypothetical situation:
I got into both RVU (DO granting program) and SGU (Caribbean MD program)
I asked which program I should attend to be most competitive for their residency program.
31/40 Said I should I should attend RVU
2/40 Said that IMG MDs and DOs are looked at equally
7/40 never responded.
0/40 Suggested SGU
I think that speaks pretty loudly."

It is a simple matter of fact that attending a US school (whether MD or DO) will give you an easier time during the ACGME residency match. It really isn't that hard to get into a USDO school in terms of hard stats. But the benefits of attending one will be apparent when residency application time comes around. If you have the stats to be enrolled in a Caribbean, or Irish, or Australian school, then you shouldn't have a problem getting into a USDO school either.

Section 7: Canadian friendly American osteopathic medical schools

Michigan State University - College of Osteopathic Medicine (MSUCOM)
Website: http://com.msu.edu/
Rating: very Canadian friendly

MSUCOM is currently in the seventh year of their **Canadian initiative** - the intent to recruit 20-25 qualified Canadian students each year over the next several years to help promote the growth of osteopathic medicine in Canada. MSUCOM currently has the largest number of Canadians attending a DO institution in the continental US. The Canadian Initiative has been a great success, and MSUCOM easily ranks as the most sought after DO medical school by Canadian applicants.

MSUCOM has taken the initiative to recruit qualified Canadian applicants and will be setting a special tuition rate for these students - Canadian matriculants will be given $20,000 a year scholarship for each of the four years they are at MSUCOM.

It should also be noted that MSUCOM bases their acceptance solely on the application. For the most part, no interview is required for acceptance to this school.

Western University of Health Sciences - College of Osteopathic Medicine of the Pacific (WUHS-COMP)
Website: www.westernu.edu
Rating: very Canadian friendly

Why was WUHS-COMP my first choice?

Living in California is a privilege that few people get to experience. You are also around 1-2 hours away from beaches, deserts, ski resorts, disneyland, universal studio, and only four hours away from Las Vegas. Given the competitive nature of the application process, and also the draw of the geography, I think anyone who gets an acceptance to Western lucky.

Marian University College of Osteopathic Medicine (MU-COM)
Website: www.marian.edu/osteopathic-medical-school
Rating: very Canadian friendly

- Many Canadians were recently accepted since the inception of this school.

Lincoln Memorial University - DeBusk College of Osteopathic Medicine (LMU - DCOM)
Website: www.lmunet.edu/dcom/
Rating: Canadian friendly

Kansas City University of Medicine and Biosciences (KCUMB)
Website: **www.kcumb.edu**
Rating: Canadian friendly

Strengths of KCUMB (courtesy of Lynda Simpson - KCUMB Class of 2015):

- KCUMB has a systems based curriculum from day one. This appealed to me because I didn't like the idea of a solid block of anatomy or biochemistry (mind numbing) and then having to map it back to a system in second year.
- The teaching staff at KCUMB are fantastic. They all pretty much go out of their way to ensure you understand the material, many come up with creative ways to help you learn the material, and all are available for extra help whenever you need it.
- All teaching material and tests are now electronically based, so they give everyone an iPad during 1st year and an iPad mini at the start of 3rd year. During 3rd year we have access to UptoDate and Epocrates through KCUMB, and now an iPad mini to access it.
- Clinical exposure starts right away and you get to practice on classmates, "plastic patients", "actor patients", and children attending KC Public Schools through the KCUMB Score One programs that provides school physicals to children in underserved neighbourhoods.
- The general philosophy of the school is to give back to the community in which the school is based. This area is one of the poorer neighbourhoods of Kansas City and the

residents really appreciate all that school contributes to the community.

- KCUMB has been investing in upgrading a lot of the infrastructure and buildings at KCUMB to ensure that students have access to the latest technology and places to learn that are environmentally efficient, safe, secure, and relaxing.
- KCUMB consistently has a very high step / level 1 board pass rate - always above the national average (90%+ depending on the year). Similar pass rates for step / level 2, PE, and 3.

Weaknesses:

- Since the neighbourhood that KCUMB is quite poor, it unfortunately attracts an undesirable element. There is a strong security presence at all hours, and I never had an issue, but it isn't the neighbourhood to take chances in by taking a stroll at night by yourself.
- I would have liked to have more time allocated to studying for step 1/ level 1 boards at the end of first year. We technically had about a month after classes ended, but even then there were odds and ends that had to wrapped up so we had extraneous mandatory meetings that could have been scheduled earlier or handled via online learning.

University of New England College of Osteopathic Medicine (UNECOM)

Website: **www.une.edu/com**

Rating: Canadian friendly

- Must complete all prerequisites at latest the December before your commencing year.

Nova Southeastern University College of Osteopathic Medicine (NSU - COM)
Website: **http://osteopathic.nova.edu/**
Rating: Canadian friendly

- NSU - COM is located in Fort Lauderdale in Florida. It is a very popular school, so apply early!

Chicago College of Osteopathic Medicine (CCOM)
Website:
https://www.midwestern.edu/programs_and_admission/il_osteopathic_medicine.html
Rating: Canadian friendly

Arizona College of Osteopathic Medicine (AZCOM)
Website: **https://www.midwestern.edu/programs-and-admission/az-osteopathic-medicine.html**
Rating: very Canadian friendly

- Beware of their $300k escrow account request.

Touro College of Osteopathic Medicine - New York (TouroCOM- NY)
Website: **http://tourocom.touro.edu/**
Rating: Canadian friendly

- Very minority friendly with many Canadian matriculants over the years.

Schools that have accepted few Canadians in the past:

Lake Erie College of Osteopathic Medicine (LECOM)
Lake Erie College of Osteopathic Medicine Bradenton Campus (LECOM Bradenton)

Website: **www.lecom.edu/**
Rating: Possible given individual circumstances

- I have only known of one Canadian who matriculated at this school.

Pennsylvania College of Osteopathic Medicine (PCOM) / PCOM - GA (Georgia campus)
Website: **www.pcom.edu/**
Rating: not Canadian friendly

- Canadians rarely if ever receive invitations for interview at this school. The only Canadians admitted to PCOM were dual citizens.

Kirksville College of Osteopathic Medicine (KCOM)
Website: **www.atsu.edu/kcom/**
Rating: Possible given individual circumstances

- The Kirksville College of Osteopathic Medicine was the founding school of osteopathic medicine in the 1800s. Unfortunately, KCOM is not very Canadian friendly. There were only one or two Canadians who matriculated in this school over the past four years.

Schools that accept international applicants:

University of North Texas Health Science Center at Fort Worth/ Texas College of Osteopathic Medicine (UNTHSC/TCOM)
Website: **https://www.unthsc.edu/texas-college-of-osteopathic-medicine/**
Rating: Possible given individual circumstances

- The Texas medical school application system is separate from the AACOM, but Canadians have been known to be accepted to this school.

William Carey University College of Osteopathic Medicine (WCUCOM)
Website:
http://www.wmcarey.edu/departments/college-osteopathic-medicine

Arkansas College of Osteopathic Medicine (ARCOM)
Website: **http://arcomedu.org/**

Burrell College of Osteopathic Medicine (BCOM) at New Mexico State University
Website: **https://bcomnm.org/**

Liberty University College of Osteopathic Medicine (LUCOM)
Website: **http://www.liberty.edu/lucom/**

Section 8: National level exam requirements and how to remain in the US after medical school

What kinds of examinations are required?

Osteopathic medical schools have their own set of board exams. These are the **COMLEX exams**. There are four COMLEX exams, **COMLEX level I, COMLEX level II CE (cognitive evaluation), COMLEX II level PE (Performance evaluation), and COMLEX level III**.

Taking the COMLEX series allow you to apply for AOA (American Osteopathic Association) residency spots. Many ACGME (MD) residencies will also accept

COMLEX scores instead of USMLE scores for purposes of application to ACGME residencies as a DO. These residencies typically are in primary care such as family medicine, internal medicine, psychiatry, and paediatrics. The more competitive the specialty, the more likely that they will require both the COMLEX and USMLE, or only the USMLE.

As an American osteopathic medical student, requirement for graduation is successful completion of COMLEX level I, COMLEX level II CE, and COMLEX level II PE. The COMLEX level III is not a graduation requirement.

However, if you want to return to Canada, you ***must*** match into ACGME (MD) residencies. Taking the USMLEs (for DO students) is only to show residency programs that you are competitive. Many programs will accept the COMLEX. Others will require USMLE Step 1. The USMLE Step 2 is usually optional but can help ACGME program directors determine your skills and strengths.

Alternatively, there are dual accredited AOA/ACGME residencies; they take either the COMLEX or the USMLEs.

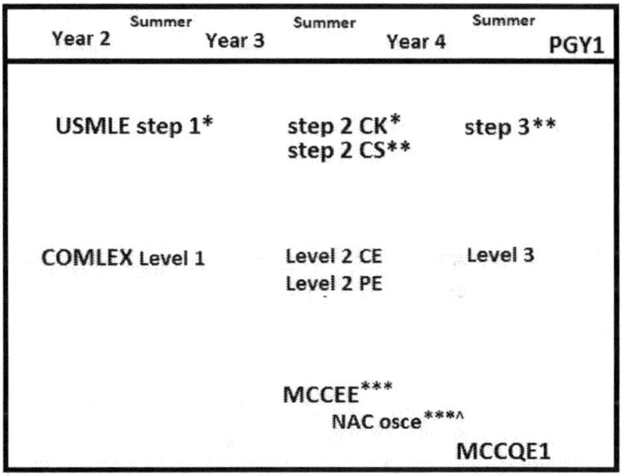

*optional but recommended

** optional

*** required for IMGs and US DOs

***^ required for IMGs and US DOs, except for Quebec

Figure 4. Basic timeline of the national level exams recommended to be taken as a Canadian DO.

At the present time, COMSA and the COA strongly encourage Canadians to take both the COMLEX and USMLEs (at least the USMLE step 1 and Step 2 CK). This is because the COMLEX is required for graduation from a DO medical school while the USMLEs are sometimes required and usually very helpful to one's application to ACGME residencies. Lastly, Canada only recognizes ACGME residencies - so it is very helpful for the Canadian trained DO to take the USMLEs to make themselves more competitive for US ACGME programs.

Here is a basic order in which these exams can be written as a Canadian DO student. It is designed to maximize both your chances of matching in the US and Canada. If you are not interested in the Canadian match, simply ignore the MCCEE and NAC OSCE. This is all the board exam information you need to know as a pre-med. For a complete discussion on the tests, strategies and details needed to succeed as a medical student, see **Part two - Section 12: How to succeed in the preclinical years - strategies for standardized tests**

How competitive are ACGME residencies?

The competitiveness of ACGME residencies depend on the discipline and the level of specialization or rarity of that discipline. In general, specialty residencies are difficult (e.g. radiology, orthopaedics, anaesthesiology, dermatology), whereas primary care residencies (e.g. family medicine, psychiatry, paediatrics) are easier to match into.

In order to match in the US in a **competitive** specialty residency, you need to dominate the **USMLE Step 1**, which is the single most important factor in getting residency interview invites **(the USMLE step 2 CK is nearly as important).**

If you have an average score on the USMLE Step 1 (e.g., a 220), combined with your Canadian background (i.e., requiring visa sponsorship), these two factors are probably enough to sink your application to a competitive specialty in the US.

If you are interested in primary care residencies, then having average or even slightly below average USMLE scores will suffice.

In addition, ACGME residencies also care greatly about your **clinical grades**, and your **letters of recommendations**. Even so, most residency programs will use an arbitrary minimum USMLE Step 1 score as a **cut-off**, depending on the competitiveness of the application pool for that year. If you do not make the cut-off, your application will be instantly rejected, regardless of your clinical grades.

Can I practice in Canada after US ACGME accredited residency training?

The simplest answer is "yes", but with a number of conditions.

Most ACGME accredited specialty residencies are shorter than their Canadian equivalents. For example, obstetrics & gynaecology, ophthalmology, psychiatry, PM&R, pathology, dermatology, and anaesthesiology are all **four** year residencies in the US. They are all **five** year residencies in Canada. Most emergency medicine residencies in the US are **three** years, with some being **four** years. The complete Canadian Royal College emergency medicine residency is **five** years. Internal medicine and paediatrics take **three** years in the US. In Canada, these are **four** year residencies. Only radiology is both **five** years in Canada and the US.

Even for Canadian medical graduates, their Canadian postgraduate training must be assessed by the **Royal College** before they are eligible to take the Royal College exams to be certified as a specialist (1). For Canadians with ACGME accredited training, they must apply for an **assessment of their ACGME residency training** (2).

If your ACGME accredited training is in a **surgical specialty (i.e., general surgery, cardiac surgery, neurosurgery, orthopaedic surgery, otolaryngology —head and neck surgery, plastic surgery, or urology)**, then **in addition** to the assessment of your ACGME residency training, you must also successfully complete the **Surgical Foundations**

exam to be eligible for the final exams in your surgical specialty.

After the assessment, due to the discrepancy in length of training between ACGME and Royal College programs, an additional year of training (usually in the form of a fellowship) will need to be completed before meeting Royal College training requirements (3). An additional year of training may not be needed for radiology due to the same length of training in the US and Canada.

On the contrary, while family medicine is only **two** years in Canada, it is **three** years in the US. The **College of Family Physicians of Canada (CFPC)** has a **reciprocity agreement** with the **American Board of Family Medicine (ABFM)** to recognize ACGME family medicine training (4), without the need to take the Certification Examination in Family Medicine (CCFP).

References:

(1)http://www.royalcollege.ca/rcsite/credentials-exams/exam-eligibility-e
Accessed January 26th 2017.

(2)http://www.royalcollege.ca/rcsite/credentials-exams/exam-eligibility/assessment-route/applicants-acgme-training-in-us-e
Accessed January 26th 2017.

(3)http://www.royalcollege.ca/rc/faces/oracle/webcenter/portalapp/pages/ibd.jspx?_adf.ctrl-state=apqmevzc2_39&_afrLoop=2528561114380526 6&_afrWindowMode=0&_afrWindowId=apqmevzc2_49#!
Accessed January 26th 2017.

(4) http://www.cfpc.ca/RecognizedTraining/
Accessed January 26th 2017.

What if I want to stay in the US for residency?

In order to stay in the United States for graduate medical education, you need to have either one of two visas. One is the "J" visa (also called the **J-1**), and the other is the "H" visa (also called the **H1b**).

The J Visa:

The J visa is an "exchange visitors" visa. The idea is that you get to come to the US for training, and then take that training back to your home country to improve the health care / teaching in your home country. I believe J visas are only available for clinical medicine and medical research. The basic facts are as follows:

1. It is easy to get. There is no limit to the number of J visas issued. The ECFMG is the sole source of these visa in the US. **(http://www.ecfmg.org/evsp/index.html)**

2. In order to get this visa, you need:
    1. To obtain an **ECFMG certification**
    2. Pass Step I and Step II CK of the USMLE (Or the COMLEX equivalent)
    3. Obtain a contract for a PGY position in the US
    4. Provide a **Statement of Need** from the Ministry of Health of the country of most recent legal permanent residence, regardless of country of citizenship. This statement provides written assurance that the country needs physicians trained in the proposed specialty and/or subspecialty. It also serves to confirm the applicant physician's commitment to return to that country upon completion of training in the United States.

3. The **statement of need** is obtained from **Health Canada**.

4. The fees for these visas are inexpensive, and no lawyer is required.

5. Spouses / children obtain a J-2 visa, which allows them to work/study in any capacity (i.e. they are a full work visa)

6. The visa holder is required to return to their home country (i.e. Canada) for a minimum of 2 years after the visa expires.

7. The only exception to this rule is the **J Visa Waiver program** -- if a J Visa physician obtains a job which qualifies for a waiver, and they work in that position for a certain period of time (usually 3 years), they become exempted from the "return home" requirement. These positions are rare, often poorly compensated, and potentially less than ideal. They only exist because US physicians will not fill them.

8. You cannot moonlight on a J visa.

9. A J visa is only good for 6 years. This covers most residencies and fellowships.

10. You can only change specialties once on a J visa, before the end of the PGY-2 year.

The H Visa:

An H visa is a true work visa. It allows a non-US citizen to hold a professional position which requires significant training. H visas are commonly used by physicians and by IT professionals. Because of the "Home Country" issue with the J visa, they are often preferred by non-US citizens training in the US. However, they have some other issues. Basic facts:

1. They are much more difficult to get. There is an annual cap (i.e. limit) to the number of H visa's

available in the US. However, nonprofits and universities are immune to the cap, and hence can always get an H1B visa.

2. H1B visas are much more expensive and complicated. There is a ~$1000 premium processing fee, which really isn't optional if you want to start your training anywhere near July 1st. This site (http://www.immihelp.com/visas/h1b/h1b-visa-requirements.html) has a list of all the documents / paperwork you will need to generate.
3. Some residency programs refuse to sponsor H visas because of all of the work involved.
4. If you are an IMG who studied outside the US or a CMG from a Canadian medical school, in order to get an H1B, you will need to pass all **three** steps of the USMLE (unlike the J, where you only need Step 1 and 2 CK). Luckily for non-US citizens at American medical schools, there is no requirement for completing the USMLE series before the H1B can be offered. **US DO candidates can also use the COMLEX series instead of the USMLE series for H1B sponsorship.**
5. If you get hired in the US into a permanent job (i.e. **not** residency) on an H visa, your employer can sponsor you for permanent residency. This is one of the easiest paths to citizenship.
6. Your H visa is only good for 6 years (actually it's good for 3 years, and renewable once). This can be a big problem if you decide to do a complex fellowship (like interventional cardiology, which is 3+3+2 = 8 years in most institutions now).

7. Dependents (Spouse/children) obtain H-4 visas. They cannot work in the US on these visas.
8. You can moonlight on an H1B visa if you can obtain a full license (which depends by state).

References:

http://www.osteopathic.org/inside-aoa/development/international-osteopathic-medicine/Pages/us-visa-information.aspx
Accessed January 28th 2017.

http://www.ecfmg.org/evsp/intro-evsp.pdf
Accessed January 28th 2017.

Section 9:
How to return to Canada after completing medical school

What Canadian exams are required?

If you are a Canadian at a US MD school, then you do not need any prerequisite Canadian exams to enter the Canadian match. If you are a CSA/IMG or a Canadian at a US DO school, in order to participate in the Canadian residency match, you would need to have taken the **MCCEE** and the **NAC OSCE**.

The MCCEE and NAC OSCE are required for CSAs/IMGs or US DOs in order to participate in the Canadian match. Also, the MCCEE is a prerequisite exam for CSAs/IMGs or US DOs to be eligible to take the subsequent MCCQE part 1. Canadians from US MD schools do not need to take the MCCEE or NAC OSCE, and are eligible to take the MCCQE part 1 without a prerequisite exam.

The MCCEE is also a prerequisite exam in order to be eligible for the NAC OSCE. Currently, all Canadian provinces (except Quebec) requires USDOs and CSAs/IMGs to take the NAC OSCE as a prerequisite to application to CaRMS.

References:
http://mcc.ca/examinations/nac-overview/
Accessed January 28th 2017.
http://mcc.ca/examinations/mccee/
Accessed January 28th 2017.

Why are the MCCEE and NAC OSCE exams needed for US DO and IMG candidates but not US MD candidates?

The **Medical Council of Canada (MCC)** determines the eligibility for Canadian licensing exams. The MCC also determines the definition of what is and what is not an IMG in Canada. All IMGs as defined by the MCC are required to pass the MCCEE and NAC OSCE before partaking in CaRMS. Currently, the Medical Council of Canada defines an international medical graduate (IMG) as:

"an individual who has graduated from a medical school ***not accredited in Canada or in the US*** *(by the* ***Committee on Accreditation of Canadian Medical Schools (CACMS)*** *or by the* ***Liaison Committee on Medical Education (LCME)*** *in the US)*

or

a graduates of a US school of osteopathic medicine accredited by the ***American Osteopathic Association****"*

For the MCC, to be considered an American medical graduate or Canadian medical graduate, one must be a graduate of a medical school accredited by the

LCME or CACMS. As American osteopathic medical schools are accredited by the **Commission on Osteopathic College Accreditation (COCA)**, and not the LCME or CACMS, **the MCC considers US DO graduates to be IMGs**. Therefore, despite the fact that US DOs and US MDs are both trained in the US, often times side by side, due to ***political reasons*** pertaining to accreditation, US DOs must take the MCCEE and the NAC osce whereas US MDs do not.

References:

http://mcc.ca/about/mcc-and-route-to-licensure/
Accessed December 29th 2014.

How does the Canadian match work?

The Canadian match is divided into two parallel and separate streams. There is the CMG stream for CMGs and AMGs of LCME accredited US schools (i.e., US MD schools), and there is the IMG stream for CSAs/IMGs and USDOs.

The two parallel and separate streams also go through two iterations each year. **The first iteration of the CMG stream** includes all graduating students and prior year graduates from LCME and CACMS accredited Canadian and American schools who meet the basic eligibility criteria and have no prior postgraduate training in Canada or the US. **The first iteration of the IMG stream** is also open to graduates from international medical schools (IMGs) and COCA-accredited American DO schools who meet the basic criteria and have no prior postgraduate training in Canada or the US.

There are vastly more positions available on the first iteration of the CMG stream compared to the first iteration of the IMG stream. The number of open positions on the IMG stream only make a up a small fraction of the positions available for CMGs.

The second iteration combines the left over spots from the IMG and CMG first iteration streams, and includes positions and applicants not matched in the first iteration, as well as applicants with previous Canadian or US postgraduate training and other applicants who did not participate in the first iteration.

CMGs, US MDs, US DOs and IMGs can apply to all medical specialties available on CaRMS.

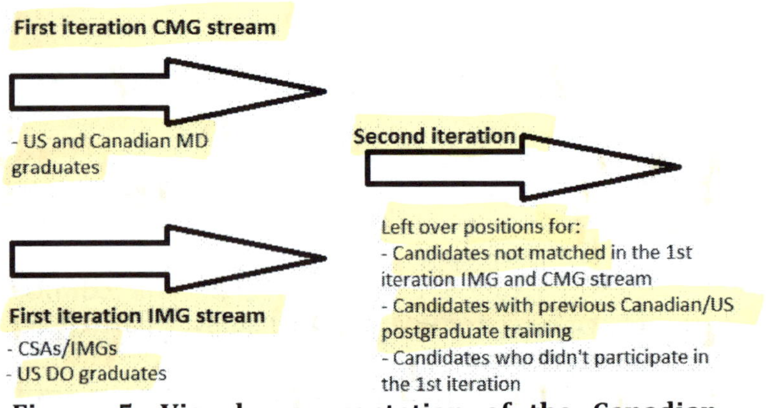

Figure 5. Visual representation of the Canadian match.

References:

http://www.carms.ca/en/residency/r-1/
Accessed January 28th 2017.

Are US DOs considered AMGs or IMGs in Canada?

In the United States, an American medical graduate is defined as graduates from a LCME accredited MD school or a COCA accredited DO school. Foreign nationals who graduate from an American medical school (whether a MD or DO school) are considered AMGs. Being an AMG has nothing to do with one's citizenship.

In Canada, the situation is more complicated. There used to be several different interpretations of what constituted a CMG or an IMG in Canada. There was the MCC definition of CMGs and IMGs, and there was the provincial definition (i.e. by the various provincial medical schools).

The Medical Council of Canada (MCC) unfortunately designates US trained DOs as IMGs because US osteopathic medical schools are accredited by the Commission on Osteopathic Colleges Accreditation (COCA), and not the LCME or CACMS (under which Canadian medical schools are accredited). The provincial definition on the other hand varied widely across the jurisdictions, with no uniform consensus.

In the provinces, the designation of US DOs varied from being considered AMGs equivalent to CMGs, to IMGs, to not even being allowed on the CaRMS match! For many years, we had the situation where US DOs were considered IMGs by the MCC, while some Canadian provinces considered them to be AMGs equivalent to CMGs, and gave them access to the first iteration CMG match. Until recently, US DOs enjoyed participation in the first iteration of the CaRMS CMG stream in British Columbia, Ontario, and for a brief period of one application cycle, Manitoba.

Unfortunately, due to the ever increasing numbers of Canadians now matriculating at American osteopathic medical schools, along with increasing numbers wanting to participate in the Canadian match, the deans of medical schools in Ontario and British Columbia had a meeting, and decided to relegate USDOs into the IMG category, in order to allow CMGs a better chance at the Canadian match.

As of 2017, the former provinces that allowed USDOs to participate in the CMG stream now only allow USDOs on the IMG stream (1). Unfortunately, as it stands, USDOs are now considered IMGs for the Canadian match.

Quebec is the exception for both IMGs and USDOs. There is only one CaRMS stream for all CMGs, AMGs and IMGs/USDOs in Quebec (unlike the parallel CMG/AMG vs. IMG streams in the rest of Canada).

Reference:

(1) Canadian Resident Matching Service (CaRMS). Provincial criteria, Ontario. Available at: http://www.CaRMS.ca/en/residency/r-1/eligibility-criteria/provincial-criteria/
Accessed January 28th 2017.

US DOs now match with IMGs in Canada, is this relevant to me?

The province of Ontario had historically been the friendliest and most receptive province for US DOs during the CaRMS match. All of the successful Canadian DO applicants matched into the province of Ontario in recent years.

Owing to the recent surge in the numbers of Canadians attending US DO schools, and the projected further increase in Canadian matriculants, Ontario and

British Columbia recently decided to change their policy towards US DOs to relegate them as IMGs. This policy became effective in 2016.

Ontario and British Columbia formerly accepted US DOs as AMGs that were considered equivalent to CMGs. However, after a few successful US DOs matched into Ontario residency programs in the CMG stream over the last few years, the deans of Ontario medical schools along with the Ontario ministry of health became concerned about the increased number of USDOs attempting to match into Ontario residency programs in the CMG stream, thereby displacing Ontario CMGs. They then decided to formally adopt the MCC definition of IMG - which had always designated USDOs as IMGs due to the differences in DO medical school accreditation in the US. More recently in 2016, British Columbia followed suit due to similar concerns, and also adopted the MCC definition of an IMG. As a result of these changes, USDOs are now effectively considered IMGs for the Canadian match.

This is a minor setback for the osteopathic profession in Canada. As stated previously, after leaving Canada for medical school, one's best chance for residency training is to match in the US. Successfully matching into Canada for residency is very challenging, and has only been accomplished by a handful of Canadian DOs who were very familiar with the Canadian matching system. By going to a US DO school, your best chance was always to match in the US, then make the arrangements to practice in Canada after US certification (should you so desire).

Only a handful of US DOs have ever managed to match into Canadian residency programs, with most of the matches in family medicine. The majority of

Canadians at US DO schools decided to stay in the US, and matched into ACGME programs.

The following is a list of known Canadian matches:

2010 - Obstetrics & gynaecology (1)
2012 - Family medicine (2)
2014 - Family medicine (2)
2015 - Internal medicine (1), psychiatry (1), family medicine (1)
2016 - Family medicine via IMG stream (1)

As can be seen since 2010, there has historically been only 1 to 3 successful US DO matches through CaRMS per year. Most were in family medicine. In light of the 2016 changes, the loss of these matches in the CMG stream does not constitute a major blow for the profession, especially when the NRMP can easily absorb the 1 to 4 graduates who will now apply to US ACGME programs.

Do US DOs possess full practice rights in Canada?

Licensure in Canada is done at the provincial level. The osteopathic physician must register with the appropriate provincial College of Physicians and Surgeons. As of 2017, US DOs have **full practice rights in all provinces and territories in Canada**. They last two provinces to update their policies were Prince Edward Island and Saskatchewan, which became official in 2016.

How do I come back to Canada?

The vast majority of Canadian students enrolled in DO institutions in the US choose to pursue an **ACGME residency** after medical school. It is also feasible and easier to complete a residency in the US, and then move back to Canada to practice medicine (while making sure to take all the Canadian licensing exams in the process).

If all the licensing exams are done, and the Canadian USDO has successfully completed an ACGME residency with the equivalent length of training indicated by the **Royal College of Physicians and Surgeons of Canada (Royal College)**, or received reciprocity with the CFPC, then the provincial colleges should grant you a full license.

The path to licensure in Canada as a DO is the same as that for a US trained MD. The only difference is the additional board exams we have to take (i.e., the COMLEX series) and the MCCEE (in addition to the USMLEs, and MCCQEs).

Can US DOs find employment in Canadian hospitals?

In Canada, there are board certified USDOs in the fields of internal medicine, anaesthesiology, psychiatry, obstetrics and gynaecology, emergency medicine. These fields require hospital privilege, and one can see that hospitals will not discriminate based on one's medical degree, especially if there are provincial legislature that states the USDO degree being equivalent to the MD degree.

As long as the USDO is able to obtain provincial licensure (which includes board certification either through the **CFPC** or the **Royal College**), all medical career paths are open to you in Canada.

"The world under heaven, after a long period of division, tends to unite; after a long period of union, tends to divide. This has been so since antiquity."

— Romance of the Three Kingdoms
Luo Guan Zhong (1330–1400)

Section 10:
The AOA and ACGME merger

Forces of integration vs. forces of separation

There are forces present that tend to better integrate the DO and MD worlds. For example, the AACOM announced in 2011 that the AAMC is opening its **Visiting Student Application Service (VSAS)** to osteopathic medical schools/osteopathic medical students beginning in 2012 (1).

The VSAS is the electronic elective rotation application service used by US allopathic schools. Before, DOs and IMGs did not have access to it, but in 2012, DOs will (whereas IMGs still have to use paper and pencil applications). Basically, this means that DOs will have greater access to opportunities available in the

MD world, and greater success at obtaining ACGME residencies.

As well, there are forces present that want to keep osteopathic medicine as a distinct but equal and parallel world). For example, the COMLEX and USMLE exams will not merge anytime soon. However, the forces of integration are also present such that most of the primary care residencies will recognize the COMLEX exams as equivalent to the USMLEs, and will take the COMLEX in lieu of the USMLEs (so in a lot of cases, the DO can get away with not writing the USMLEs, and still end up going to an ACGME residency).

(1) Visiting Student Application Service
https://services.aamc.org/20/vsas/
Accessed January 25th 2017.

AOA and ACGME Agree to Single GME Accreditation System

On Feb 26th, 2014, the AOA and the ACGME agreed to a unified system of residency training for all US MD and DO graduates. The AOA statement was as follows:

"After months of discussion, the AOA, along with the Accreditation Council for Graduate Medical Education (ACGME) and the American Association of Colleges of Osteopathic Medicine (AACOM), have agreed to a ***single accreditation system for graduate medical education programs in the United States.***

A single graduate medical education (GME) accreditation system will evaluate and provide accountability for the competency of physician residents consistently across all

GME programs. This ensures the quality and efficiency of postdoctoral education, while preserving the unique dimensions of the osteopathic medical profession and recognizing its contribution to health care in the U.S.

Under the agreement:

From July 1, 2015 to June 30, 2020, AOA-accredited training programs will transition to ACGME recognition and accreditation.

*There will continue to be **osteopathic-focused training programs under the ACGME accreditation system**. Two osteopathic review committees will be developed to evaluate and set standards for the osteopathic aspects of training programs seeking osteopathic recognition.*

***DOs and MDs would have access to all training programs.** There will be prerequisite competencies and a recommended program of training for MD graduates who apply for entry into osteopathic-focused programs.*

AOA and AACOM will become ACGME member organizations, and each will have representation on ACGME's board of directors.

The agreement provides the framework for the osteopathic and allopathic communities to prepare future generations of physicians with the highest quality graduate medical education and serve as a unified voice for graduate medical education resources to help mitigate the primary care physician shortage and better serve the public."

This is a great achievement for all DOs, and it is especially a great thing for Canadians at US DO schools. The separate identities of the AOA and ACGME had been a headache for the Canadian osteopathic profession for years. Canada only recognizes ACGME accredited programs. Now that the AOA and AACOM will be under the ACGME umbrella, and all AOA programs will transition to ACGME accreditation or be closed down, this will have wide ramifications for Canadians. All Canadian graduates of US DO programs will essentially transition to ACGME post graduate training by 2020, which fits precisely the criteria needed to return to Canada.

Will it get harder for DOs?

A question that was presented to me was, "will it actually get harder for DOs since AOA programs can now take MDs? Doesn't it increase the competitiveness for AOA residencies without decreasing the competitiveness of ACGME residencies?"

I doubt it. Things will get better this way. For instance, a lot of these competitive AOA specialties like orthopaedics, emergency medicine, anaesthesiology were closed to Canadians because they were not ACGME accredited, and Canadian DOs cannot come back to Canada had they gone to these programs. Now, with the merger, Canadian DOs can go to these formerly AOA residencies and still come to Canada afterwards because they will all be ACGME programs by 2020. These formerly AOA specialty programs are still run by DOs, so they might still have a preference for their own in exactly the same way that specialty MD programs have a preference for MDs in the upper echelons.

As for visas, it seems the formerly AOA programs are at least J1 sponsoring (which was an issue before because a Canadian in such an AOA program had to come back to Canada after graduation for 2 years, and their AOA training wasn't recognized). Now with the merger, the J1 visa is no longer as much an issue because the AOA program is now ACGME accredited, and they can in theory come back to Canada to practice as ACGME training is recognized.

Also, a stipulation is that for a MD to match into a formerly AOA program, they have to have some additional training in the osteopathic arts (i.e., OMM). As for how many MDs will actually take the effort to do additional training in OMM in order to match into a formerly AOA specialty, who knows! Only time will tell.

What does this merger mean for US MDs and IMGs?

I think this is a win-win-win situation for MDs, DOs, and IMGs alike.

MDs can now theoretically match into formerly AOA residencies and specialties. They'll be asked to do some additional training in DO specific OMM and related medicine, which will hopefully migrate that area of medicine into the allopathic world.

IMGs now in theory have access to a few thousand additional primary care and formerly AOA residencies, many of which went unfilled in the past. In light of the relatively stagnant numbers of residency programs and ever increasing numbers of medical graduates coming into the US, this merger will hopefully temporarily slow down the crunch against them.

Section 11:
What's in store for the future?

The following was contributed by the late Dr. Fiddler - former President of the Ontario chapter of the Canadian Osteopathic Association.

As a Canadian osteopathic physician with an unrestricted license in Canada since 1987 , and one who has been actively involved in obtaining full unrestricted licensure in Canada since 1979, I believe I can provide some valuable insight into where the osteopathic profession is in Canada and where it is going.

When I entered osteopathic medical school in 1979 D.O.s in Canada were on the verge of extinction. They were limited to manipulative medicine, and there was a recent government report that indicated that Canada had too many physicians. Medical school class sizes were being decreased and access to licensure for foreign physicians was being curtailed. There was little appetite to change things for the osteopathic profession.

In spite of this, numerous letters were sent to all Canadian licensing bodies, federal/provincial governments, the Medical Council of Canada, and the Royal College of Physicians and Surgeons of Canada resulting ultimately in full unrestricted licensure in Alberta, Ontario and British Columbia.

Essentially for most of the past 25 years, only four fully licensed osteopathic physicians have this organization (the Canadian Osteopathic Association) alive. Although each of us has been fully licensed, with nothing to gain for ourselves we have worked hard to achieve what each of you if accepted to a D.O. school will benefit from.

U.S. trained osteopathic physicians have been recognized by each of the Medical Council of Canada, the Royal College of Physicians and Surgeons of Canada, the Canadian College of Family Physicians, and CaRMS in addition to the **Federation of Medical Regulatory Authorities of Canada (FPMRAC)** (composed of registrars of each provincial medical licensing authority).

Things have changed. When I returned to Canada even after completing an ACGME accredited residency in internal medicine I had to do one year of a rotating internship. Subsequently I was accepted to a fellowship but this was rescinded after the Royal College learned about my underlying degree. Not now. You can practice in Canada now without prejudice. I have never encountered it professionally. FPMRAC as a result of the Agreement on Internal Trade has recognized the American D.O. degree as equivalent to the allopathic (M.D.) degree. This means that you will be able to practise throughout Canada fully licensed as a D.O. (as of 2017).

To those of you that are already accepted. Now is the time to work towards making your future in Canada even better. With respect this must be done in a professional manner as now you are a professional. I believe that the Canadian students need to organize to address the issues they face, issues that are not nearly as challenging as in the past. The wheel does not need to be re-invented. We want thoughtful discussion on issues and coordinated planning to attack each of the issues that affect your future. The Canadian Osteopathic Association would like to help facilitate organizing the Canadian students so that we can pass the torch on responsibly to the leaders of tomorrow.

As Canadian osteopathic students you now have the responsibility not only to be the best for your patients but also to be the best physician you can be as you will be Ambassadors of the Osteopathic profession In Canada. May your idealism of today, transcend throughout your careers.

What has being done to increase awareness of osteopathic medicine in Canada?

As a profession, what we suffered in the past was a chronic shortage of Canadians who bothered to matriculate at US DO schools, and subsequently, a shortage of US trained Canadian DOs who came back to Canada. As such, there was a lack of brand recognition in Canada for DOs, as the non-doctor variety of DO osteopaths still outnumber US trained DO physicians. This is common knowledge amongst the Canadian DO physician community, and we have done many things over the years to remedy this issue, and to increase the public awareness of the DO "brand" in Canada.

Ongoing advocacy and public education by the COA and COMSA

In the past two years or so, Canadian DO students have formed an advocacy group to raise the awareness of osteopathic medicine in Canada.

The Canadian Osteopathic Medical Student Association (COMSA) is dedicated to spreading awareness of osteopathic medicine throughout Canada, and helping Canadians realize their dream of practicing medicine. Our activities range from advocacy of Canadian regulatory bodies and policy makers for increased accessibility of osteopathic physicians to practice opportunities in Canada, to matching Canadian pre-meds with osteopathic physicians in Canada for shadowing and letters of recommendation, and researching and compiling information about applying to DO school and returning to Canada.

More recently, COMSA has been invited by Canadian universities to host seminars to reach of an ever growing audience of pre-medical students. Starting in 2013, COMSA has successfully completed seminars at the **University of Waterloo, University of Toronto, Ryerson University, McGill University, University of British Columbia, Simon Fraser University, and the University of Calgary**. We plan to make these seminars an annual event, to be presented by newly matriculated first and second year Canadian DO students. Our audience is growing and our advocacy efforts are ongoing. We have seen a steady increase in interest and public knowledge of US DO schools amongst the Canadian pre-medical student population.

The attempt to create an osteopathic medical school in Canada

In the mid 2000s at the inaugural meeting of the Osteopathic International Alliance in Washington D.C., members of the Canadian Osteopathic Association approached a number of U.S. osteopathic medical schools to see if there was interest in developing a satellite osteopathic medical school in Canada. They did this with the intent of trying to expeditiously increase the number of osteopathic physicians in Canada.

Of the several schools that were interested, they pursued Michigan State University - College of Osteopathic medicine (MSUCOM) due to its brand recognition and reputation. They felt that this would be best to help our cause In Canada. MSUCOM was unique because of its status as a U.S. land grant institution, and facilitating expansion of a satellite osteopathic medical campus in Canada would fit its mandate.

Ultimately, an osteopathic medical school was not established in Canada due to the extremely small numbers of DO physicians in Canada, and the general lack of knowledge that the Canadian public had relating to US trained osteopathic physicians. For the present time, the idea of an osteopathic medical school in Canada is far from being realized.

However, having attempted to create an osteopathic medical school in Canada, the profession became acutely aware of the lack of brand recognition in Canada. Something had to be done to address the dwindling numbers of US trained Canadian DOs in Canada. With that in mind, an agreement was reached with MSUCOM to start the **Canadian initiative** where MSUCOM has agreed to accept 25 Canadians per year for the next several years to get a jumpstart on a nucleus of osteopathic physicians in Ontario.

What is the future of Canadian medical school entrance?

Here are the predictions I have for future pre-meds. Canadian medical school entrance will continue to have a strong regional preference in the majority of provinces. Medical school entrance in Canada will continue to be extremely difficult, forcing hundreds of Canadians to look for American or overseas options for medical education every year. More and more Canadians will come to the conclusion that it is better to attend an American medical school (MD or DO) than to become a CSA. Even so, Canadians will continue to attend American and international medical schools in record numbers.

For many years, Canadians have missed a great opportunity by not being aware of American D.O. medical schools. Things are rapidly changing now, and there is a surge of Canadian applicants.

The Doctors of Osteopathic Medicine (DO) program provides an additional pathway for students interested pursuing a medical education. The additional benefits associated with a DO degree, including securing proper post-graduate training in the US will continue to encourage more Canadian students to apply to an osteopathic medical school versus other IMG routes. Given the already increasing trend of Canadian enrollment in US osteopathic medical schools and the ongoing advocacy of osteopathic education, it is to be expected that Canadian medical programs will continue to be exposed osteopathic medical doctors. It is therefore advisable for current Canadian pre-med students to gain awareness of osteopathic trained physicians.

More DO graduates are matching into ACGME residencies and specialty programs. This trend has been going on for over a decade and there are no signs of it slowing down. I can't stress enough that the experiences in a DO medical school will be mostly identical to one who experienced an American MD medical school. The absolute advantages of being an AMG with vastly better match rates, better student visas, education quality, and living quality in the US all make it worthwhile to pursue this route in comparison to the international options.

"When you have attained the way of strategy, there will be nothing that you cannot understand. You will see the way in everything."

- The Book of Five Rings,
Miyamoto Musashi (1584 - 1645)

Part Two

What you need to know as a medical student studying outside Canada

Introduction:

So you have been accepted into medical school, or even finished the first year or two. Congratulations! If no one has said it to you already, give yourself a pat on the back! Good job! You have come a long way. Feel proud that you have come this far!

You are probably thinking, I have passed all my first year courses, and are about to finish second year (or beyond), what should I expect or do now? Well, you've come to the right place!

Everything that I will impart on you comes from my own personal experience of going through 4 years of medical school in the US system, writing the boards (3 sets! USMLE, COMLEX, AND MCC exams), going through the ERAS match, as well as the CaRMS match, and obtaining sixteen interviews in the US, seven interviews in Canada.

I only applied to family medicine (as that's the only specialty that interested me), so this guide will come from a perspective of family medicine.

"If you can make one heap of all your winnings
And risk it on one turn of pitch-and-toss,
And lose, and start again at your beginnings
And never breathe a word about your loss;

Yours is the Earth and everything that's in it,
And—which is more—you'll be a Man, my son!"

- Rudyard Kipling, Rewards and Fairies 1910

Section 12: How to succeed in the preclinical years - strategies for standardized tests

Board exams - succeeding in standardized tests - to USMLE or not to USMLE? (Read if you are a DO)

If you are a US MD or IMG, you need the USMLEs to graduate. It becomes trickier as a USDO. For one thing, the USMLEs are not required for graduation if you are a DO. So it is mainly taken to embellish a DO's application if they were applying to ACGME residencies. That said, a lot of ACGME residencies don't even require the USMLEs to be taken if you are a DO who has applied to their program.

Experiential pearl:

For family medicine, that certainly was the case. I have examined hundreds of programs, and I have only seen one program that asks for the USMLEs. All the other programs were perfectly fine with just the COMLEX series as your credential when applying to their program.

For family medicine as a DO, you can most likely get away with taking only the COMLEX and not touching the USMLEs. This can also work for paediatrics, and psychiatry, and basically most of the primary care specialties. Not taking the USMLE has no ramifications for Canada as well. Taking the USMLEs has no bearing on whether you can write the MCC exams (i.e., MCCEE, QEI, QEII). The USMLEs is simply not part of the evaluation process for residency matching in Canada.

However, as Canadians studying in the U.S., it is advised that we take the USMLEs in addition to the COMLEX to stand out during residency matching, and to have a stronger application for residency.

I took both the COMLEX and USMLEs. I took the USMLEs step 1, and step 2 CK. I did not take the USMLE step 2 CS or step 3. In fact, I had planned to obtain US licensure through the COMLEX pathway, with the USMLEs step 1 and step 2 CK mainly to bolster my residency application.

COMLEX timeline

COMLEX part 1

- It is a test of the basic medical sciences. Written in the summer after the end of your second year.

- Registering for the COMLEX requires verification from your college of osteopathic medicine. Some schools will not let you register without first completing a practice exam - the COMSAE.
- The cost and timing of the COMLEX I are similar to the USMLE Step 1.
- The material covered is the same as the USMLE Step 1, with the addition of OMM principles which are only tested on the COMLEX. The style of questions is somewhat different as well.

COMLEX part 2

- The COMLEX level 2 Clinical Exam (CE) is similar in content to the USMLE Step 2 CK, with the addition of OMM principles.
- It is a test of clinical medicine. Written at the end of your third year (if a low Step 1 score needs to be boosted by a strong Step 2), or sometime in your fourth year, usually in the spring after interviews (if you don't want to risk getting a lower score than Step 1 if you scored highly).

COMLEX Step 3

- Typically written at the end of PGY-1.
- It tests the knowledge of clinical concepts and principles needed to solve medical problems as independently practicing physicians.

COMPLETE INFORMATION on the COMLEX Exams: http://www.nbome.org/comlex-cbt.asp

FEE Information:
http://www.nbome.org/exams-fees.asp

USMLE timeline

USMLE Step 1

- It is a test of the basic medical sciences. Written in the summer after the end of Med 2.
- Register in December of second year to take the USMLE step 1 at some point between May and December.
- Most people take the test in May or June.
- Assesses the understanding and application of basic sciences. Necessary for most ACGME programs.

USMLE Step 2

- The clinical knowledge (CK) portion is multiple choices; the clinical skills (CS) portion is a practical exam.
- Step 2 is reportedly easier than step 1
- It is a test of clinical medicine. Written at the end of Med 3 (if a low Step 1 score needs to be boosted by a strong Step 2) or sometime in Med 4, usually in the spring after interviews (if you don't want to risk getting a lower score than Step 1 if you scored highly).

USMLE Step 3

- You have seven years to complete all three steps of the USMLE from the time you pass the Step 1.
- Step 3 can be taken during the first year of residency.
- Assesses the ability to apply medical knowledge and clinical science in the unsupervised practice of medicine.
- It is typically written at the end of PGY-1. Many states require you to have completed 6 months or a full year of internship/residency as a

prerequisite, although if you register for this exam through certain states (ie. California, Connecticut), you may take it immediately after med school graduation before having started your PGY-1 year, even if your PGY-1 year is in a different state.

The USMLE exams can be registered here:
http://www.usmle.org/apply/

FEE Information:
http://www.nbme.org/students/examfees.html

Medical Council of Canada (MCC) Exams:
MCCEE:

The **Medical Council of Canada Evaluating Examination (MCCEE)** is a four-hour, computer-based examination offered in both English and French at more than 500 centres in 80 countries worldwide. International medical graduates, international medical students in their final clinical year and U.S. osteopaths must take the MCCEE as a prerequisite for eligibility to the MCC Qualifying Examinations, as well as Canadian residency matching.

The content of the MCCEE is most similar to the USMLE step 2 CK, and is also comparable to difficulty to the COMLEX II CE. Adequate preparation of for the USMLE step 2 CK and COMLEX II CE would be sufficient to pass the MCCEE.

If you intend to enter the Canadian Match for a PGY1 position immediately following graduation, CaRMS requires your MCCEE score by November of your 4th year. Because the MCCEE is only offered five times a year, this means that the test must be taken no later than the September block of the year you hope to apply. The application process for the MCCEE is long and expensive, so being organized and informed is crucial to your success in entering the CaRMS match.

The information for scheduling of the MCCEE is constantly being updated. It is to your benefit to frequently check on the Medical Council of Canada website for updates in policy and scheduling: **www.mcc.ca**.

The NAC OSCE:

The NAC OSCE is a recently added test required for CaRMS. All IMGs applying to CaRMS will be required to take the NAC OSCE. The NAC OSCE is not a requirement for US trained MDs.

Since late 2016, CaRMS decided to put all USDOs under the category of IMGs, the NAC OSCE has become a prerequisite for CaRMS application for both IMGs and USDOs.

The exception appears to be Quebec, where IMGs and USDOs continue to compete with CMGs in the CMG stream.

This exam is offered twice a year, once in March and once in September. One must have successfully passed the MCCEE before being eligible for the NAC OSCE. Therefore, one must be aware of this fact, and plan to pass their MCCEE well in advance for the NAC OSCE.

The NAC examination is not a prerequisite to obtain the Licentiate of the Medical Council of Canada (LMCC). The NAC OSCE is also not a prerequisite for eligibility to the MCCQE1 and MCCQE2 exams.

For IMGs and USDOs interested in applying to CaRMS, it is in your best interest to frequently check for updates on the NAC OSCE via: www.mcc.ca.

MCCQE Part 1

The **Medical Council of Canada Qualifying Examination Part 1 (MCCQE Part 1)** is a one-day, computer-based test that assesses the competence of candidates who have obtained their medical degree, for entry into supervised clinical practice in postgraduate training programs. The MCCQE Part I assesses knowledge, clinical skills, and attitudes as outlined by the MCC's website.

IMGs and USDOs must first have successfully passed the MCCEE before being eligible to take the MCCQE part 1.

One can take the MCCQE part 1 right after graduation. Others can take it during November of their PGY1 year. Others still choose to defer the MCCQE1 until the end of their PGY1 year.

Experiential pearl:

After completion medical school, but before graduation, I took the MCCQE part 1 and COMLEX III exams. The COMLEX III exam was relatively straight forward, and passing it meant that I was able to obtain US state licensure if I so desire in the future. As for the MCCQE part 1, I thought it was a good idea to get it out of the way, even though there is no formal rule that states that one must have passed the MCCQE part 1 before residency starts in Canada.

MCCQE Part 2

The **Medical Council of Canada Qualifying Examination Part II** assesses the competence of candidates, specifically the knowledge, skills, and attitudes essential for medical licensure in Canada prior to entry into independent clinical practice.

To be eligible for the MCCQE Part II, you must have successfully completed a minimum of twelve months of postgraduate clinical medical training.

Refer to www.mcc.ca for most up to date information regarding the MCCQE part 2.

Upcoming changes to the MCC exams

Like all national level exams, the format and mode of testing will be updated on a continual basis. The MCC exams are no different. Significant changes are coming soon (1), and it is in the best interest of medical students to keep up to date with regards to these changes.

References:

(1) http://www.mccevolution.ca/
Accessed January 25th 2017.

How do I prepare for the USMLE step 1 // COMLEX I?

The basic strategy is to use First Aid to the USMLE step 1 (make sure it's the current edition). With an empty First Aid, you will read the book and not understand most of the points. That is because you are missing the second vital part, at least a 6 month subscription to **UWORLD step 1 question bank**.

When you are doing UWORLD (ideally during the same time as you are going through the systems during second year of medical school), you should annotate all the wrong answers into your First Aid book, and also annotate notes from UWORLD onto your First Aid. If you just do UWORLD questions without any annotation, I would say that you have failed to use UWORLD correctly. By the end of your preparation period, your First Aid should be annotated to its physical limit - every empty space should be filled with notes. There should really be no empty spaces (e.g., margins, space between paragraphs) left if you have done a good job of annotation. Assuming you have done this, I suggest you go back and do uworld a **second time**. (Or, you can finish another test bank - I recommend USMLErx for the step 1).

During the last quarter of your second year, you should invest a couple days to finish **Pathoma,** an excellent supplement to your First Aid/ Uworld study routine. If done correctly, the dual First Aid/Uworld strategy should ideally get you a score of around 210 - 220 for the USMLE step 1.

I personally found that doing as many questions as possible was quite high yield. So I would recommend spending the time and money to complete more test banks than anything else. If you try to start something, **try to finish it**. It is better to have **completed** two test banks than to have started on 3 test banks but only got to 60-70% completion on all three test banks.

Maybe your foundation knowledge is really high, and the basic strategy I explained earlier will get you a score of 220-230+, I have definitely seen that happen too. Otherwise, if you have a week to two weeks left before exam day, you can consider starting one of the **Doctors In Training (DIT)** courses. I'd recommend powering through those courses after you have done your core studying (i.e., First Aid annotation and UWORLD) so that the information will stay fresh in your mind for a bit longer before test day.

You should also do some **assessment tests** before test day, at least the UWORLD assessment tests, and realize that these tests usually over predict your score by 5 - 10. Hopefully having done all three things - First Aid annotation, UWORLD, Pathoma, a learning course like DIT right before your test, you will score in the 230+ level range.

If you have done this basic strategy, you should have maybe three to five days left before your USMLE step 1 test day. In the last three to five days of your preparation, re-read your annotated First Aid over and over again. That would be like doing your test bank questions that you got wrong all over again, and is an excellent way to patch up your weaknesses. I suggest you read over your First Aid at least two to three times before test day. You should have read through that book at least five to eight times throughout your study.

How do I prepare for the OMM portion of the COMLEX?

As for the OMM portion of the COMLEX I, you can borrow/share/purchase a COMLEX test bank and simply do the OMM questions. . I only spent three days prepping for OMM, and spent the rest of the time studying the other stuff. I found that was enough to pass the OMM portion of the COMLEX.

Also, the "Green book" - **OMT Review** was also very helpful. I would purchase a copy and keep it throughout your medical career - as recertification as a DO would entail knowing OMM as well, and "OMT review" is an excellent book.

Experiential pearls:

Whatever you do, study for the USMLEs. Do not study for the COMLEX. By that I mean, if you solely study for the COMLEX, you might end up failing the USMLE and even COMLEX. But if you study for the USMLEs, you'll likely pass the USMLE, and the COMLEX as well. It is simply the way that the tests are set up -

studying for USMLEs will give you a much better foundation knowledge of medicine than studying for the COMLEX.

Strategies for the USMLE Step 2 CK // COMLEX II CE // MCCEE:

Much like studying for the USMLE step 1, studying for the USMLE step 2 CK is similar. Purchase a USMLE step 2 CK review book. I bought **First Aid Step 2 CK**. Then I purchased two test banks - **UWORLD for step 2 CK**, and **USMLErx for step 2 CK**. I completed the entire test bank of USMLErx first, before moving onto the UWORLD Step 2 CK test bank.

Along the way in third year, you will also have discipline specific shelf exams every three to four months. The **"case files"** series of books are excellent for background information. To pass or do well on these shelf exams, I completed the relevant sections for that specialty on the question banks, with constant annotation into my First Aid step 2 CK book. For example, I would read the case files book in OBGYN, do all the OBGYN questions on the USMLErx, and annotate the answers into my First Aid Step 2 CK. Before the shelf exam, I would re-read the OBGYN section of my first aid, along with all the annotation. Then I would go into the shelf exam and do relatively well.

The topics tested on the MCCEE are essentially the same material as the USMLE step 2 CK and COMLEX II CE. After preparing for the USMLE step 2 CK and COMLEX II CE, you should be ready to to pass the MCCEE.

What is the MCCEE like?

The MCCEE is more like USMLE step 2 than step 1. It is a lot easier than the USMLE step 2 CK, and about the same level of difficulty as the COMLEX II CE, or perhaps even a bit easier than COMLEX II CE. In general, there are limited test preparation resources for Canadian licensing exams. However, I used **Canadaqbank** for my preparation for the MCCEE.

Scheduling for the MCCEE

The following would apply to Canadians studying at US DO schools or international medical schools. Your third year will probably end at the end of May, beginning of June. This is when the vast majority of DOs will take their step 2 exam (COMLEX II, USMLE step 2). You probably spent the entire year studying for the USMLE step 2 CK // COMLEX II CE at this point. You will likely take your exam in between early June to August.

However, the MCCEE is scheduled around two time slots a year. The first session occurs in the Spring, with the last available date sometime in May. The next available session will be in September. This can be an issue because there is a three to four month gap between May to September. Most candidates probably won't be ready to take the MCCEE by May, they would have taken their USMLE step 2 CK exam between June to July. But there will be a good two and a half to three months gap between your US level two exams and the MCCEE, which is enough time to forget a lot of knowledge for these tests.

One more complication is the addition of the NAC OSCE for IMGs as well as USDOs. One must have a pass on the MCCEE before being eligible for the NAC OSCE. The NAC OSCE is also only offered around the Spring and Fall. One must have passed the MCCEE earlier than usual to be eligible for those provinces where NAC OSCE is required (i.e., all provinces except Quebec).

The best strategy is to frequently review the MCC website at **www.mcc.ca** for updates on scheduling, dates and policy changes for the MCCEE and NAC OSCE examinations.

Experiential pearl:

I took my USMLE step 2 exam on June 15th 2013, COMLEX II CE on July 9th 2013, and MCCEE September 14th 2013. It was a full two and a half months since the COMLEX II CE, and a full three months since the USMLE step 2 CK before I could take the MCCEE. Needless to say, I had to restudy for 5 days before I felt comfortable taking the MCCEE to score reasonably well on it.

The importance of the MCCEE score:

The MCCEE score matters for IMGs and USDOs because Canadian programs get flooded by a large number of IMGs competing for a very small pool of spots. So an objective measure in the form of the MCCEE is needed to screen out applicants. That being said, the test average for the MCCEE is 270. But the average MCCEE score for IMGs who are actually invited to interviews at Canadian programs hovers at around a 350. It is absolutely vital to score well above the average on the MCCEE to be invited to Canadian interviews.

Strategies for the COMLEX II PE and USMLE step 2 CS:

The COMLEX II PE and USMLE step 2 CS are two analogous exams. They involve standardized patient encounters with 10 different cases.

If you are a MD or IMG, then it becomes clear. You need to take the Step 2 CS to continue your education in the US. It becomes more interesting if you are a DO. For one thing, the USMLE step 2 CS is not required for graduation as a DO. But the COMLEX II PE is required for graduation.

Osteopathic medical schools will spend significant resources preparing you for the COMLEX II PE exam. You will in fact be preparing for it one way or another for the entire first three years of medical school.

The COMLEX II PE is a fairly straight forward exam. I only spent three days preparing for this exam. I read one book: **COMLEX level 2 PE review guide** by **Mark Kauffman**.

Experiential pearl:

If you fail the USMLE step 2 CS, I would argue that this is a fall that you will never recover from as a Canadian citizen trying to match in the US. You will be in the 2% of people who fail this test. This will be a red flag for all residency programs, and I have seen my friends with otherwise good stats and strong letters of recommendation not be invited to a single interview because of their failure in the USMLE step 2 CS. This is absolutely a high stakes exam, make no mistake about it.

I actually did not take the USMLE step 2 CS, I signed up for it, but cancelled the exam. I thought the stakes was too high, where a pass on the step 2 CS will not hurt me, a fail will absolutely destroy my chances at matching in the US. As such, I saw no benefit at taking the USMLE step 2 CS as a USDO who wanted family medicine.

The thing you need to know about the COMLEX PE is that of the people I know who had failed, they had failed because they were making up findings on their SOAP notes. It is not a difficult exam, almost everybody passes. However, if you did not do something during the interview, but nonetheless documented that you did that thing (i.e. false documentation), this would be grounds for an automatic fail. Always be considerate and friendly to the standardized patients, and you should be fine.

Strategies for the USMLE Step 3 // COMLEX III // MCCQE part 1:

Preparing for the USMLE step 3, COMLEX III and MCCQE part 1 is fairly straightforward. I purchased a two months' subscription to **UWORLD step 3**. I also purchased **Mastering the Boards USMLE Step 3**. I spent the least amount of time preparing for these exams out of all the previous national level board exams. Part of the reason was that I felt confident in my test taking abilities after having gone through so many national level board exams in the past.

I spent approximately two weeks preparing for the COMLEX III, and I spent approximately five days preparing for the MCCQE part 1. I passed both exams without any problems.

"Your time is limited, so don't waste it living someone else's life. Don't be trapped by dogma - which is living with the results of other people's thinking. Don't let the noise of others' opinions drown out your own inner voice. And most important, have the courage to follow your heart and intuition."

- Steve Jobs

Section 13:
How to set up elective rotations

There is no uniform way to set up your fourth year rotations. Depending on your specialty of choice and career path, the electives you choose will be different. The right collection of electives for family medicine will be totally different than the ones you would take for surgery for instance.

There are two potential ways to go about choosing fourth year electives. You could do the specialty that you like to match into over and over again. For instance, if one was interested in family medicine, they might set up most of their fourth year electives with family medicine rotations. Alternatively, they could do a few rotations in their specialty of choice, and choose to do elective rotations in a wide variety of other disciplines as a way to get exposure to the other specialties.

If you are attending medical school in the US, the first step would be to search for rotations via **VSAS**: **https://services.aamc.org/20/vsas/**.

Can elective rotations be done in Canada?

Electives can be done in Canada. The Canadian DO student must contact the Canadian medical school they are interested in, apply to that program, and then coordinate with their home school (since Canadian electives are usually considered as "**international rotations**").

The length of time that a US DO school will permit for international rotations will vary based on your school, so it is vital to be familiar with your school's international rotations policy.

Canadian DO students have successfully applied and done elective rotations at the University of Toronto, University of British Columbia, McMaster University, University of Western Ontario, and Northern Ontario School of Medicine.

Experiential Pearl:

In light of the recent changes in CaRMS, US DOs are considered IMGs in all of Canada (except Quebec). I strongly advise Canadians at US DO schools to **forego electives in Canada** after 2016, and to focus their electives at desirable US ACGME programs.

What are audition rotations?

In the US, especially in AOA programs, it is customary to do so called "audition" rotations at program sites as a way to make yourself known to the program. AOA programs care especially about audition rotations, and in many cases, is a prerequisite to get highly ranked in an AOA program. ACGME programs don't care much for audition rotations, and look at your statistics more.

Experiential pearl:

Do not feel too bad if you did an audition rotation, but received no interview from their program. This happened to me. It could be due to a lot issues beyond your control, for instance, their policy with visa sponsorship.

Electives in Canada as a US MD or DO:

If your goal is to return to Canada, then doing elective rotations in Canada in the specialty of your interest will be vital to make a return. Letters of recommendation from Canadian attendings will also be priceless for CaRMS.

As a USMD or USDO, in those Canadian schools that allow US medical students to rotate at their sites, you are allowed usually double the amount of elective time than CSAs. For instance, I was able to do 8 weeks of rotations at the University of Toronto, whereas a Canadian who went to a foreign school will only be allowed to do 4 weeks of rotations a year.

Use this time wisely. Get as many letters of recommendation as you can. Now is your time to shine, to give it your all for your return home. If your school does not have any elective rotations agreement with Canadian schools, then it is vital that you help them start this process. I was lucky that my school already had agreements with UBC and University of Toronto when I matriculated, so I didn't have to worry about doing all the paperwork to setting it up.

Experiential pearl:

In order to maximize one's chance of matching in Canada, one would need Canadian elective rotations experience. I recommend doing at least two electives (four weeks each) in Canada. This is because if your performance was subpar on one elective, you will have a chance to do well on the other. This is exactly what happened to me. I completed a family medicine rotation, did not do as well as I hoped, only got a "pass" score (a medium score in my school). For the second elective rotation, I completed an internal medicine rotation. I worked a lot harder on this rotation and impressed all the attendings. My grade for this rotation was "honors", the highest rotation score allowed by my school. I also managed to obtain three letters of recommendation from professors of medicine at the University of Toronto, which no doubt helped immensely in my bid to return to Canada.

Even being a US MD will not translate into Canadian interviews if you have not done electives in your specialty of choice in Canada. I saw exactly this scenario unfold. I met a Canadian citizen who was a US MD graduate, he applied to IM and FM for CaRMS, and did not get a single Canadian interview (even though he in theory had the 1st iteration in all Canadian provinces, and for all practical purposes, should have been considered on the same footing as a CMG). But no, he did not do Canadian electives at all, and stayed in America his entire 4 years. As such, he had no Canadian invites.

Electives in Canada as an IMG:

Many medical schools in Canada do not allow IMGs to rotate through their hospitals, or allow for a very limited single four week rotation for the entire academic year. An IMG could remedy this situation by doing **observerships**, which entails your shadowing the attending, but not being allowed to do much of anything clinically for the patient.

Regardless, observerships would still serve the purpose of obtaining letters of recommendation from Canadian attendings. Many IMGs sign up for observerships in the event that they graduated from medical school, but failed to secure a Canadian or US residency position.

Obtaining letters of recommendation (US):

Letters of recommendation from US attendings you have worked with is vital for a successful US residency application. It is to your benefit that you obtain as many letters of recommendations as possible during your third and early fourth year of medical school or while doing clinical rotations in the US.

Obtaining letters of recommendation (Canada):

It is equally important to obtain letters of recommendation from Canadian attendings for a successful CaRMS match. Usually for CMGs (those who attended medical school in Canada), there is limited objective measures to determine the competitiveness of Canadian medical graduates during residency matching. Unlike the US, Canadian medical graduates do not have to take any national level board exams like the USMLE during their four years of medical school in Canada. As such, one of the only measures where Canadian residency programs can objectively rank a Canadian graduate is the letter of recommendation from Canadian attendings.

When a Canadian studying in foreign medical schools, or Canadians studying at American medical schools apply to CaRMS, their USMLE score is not part of the evaluation process in determining the competitiveness or desirability of a candidate for a residency spot. It does not matter if someone scored a perfect score on their USMLE step 1 exam, Canadian residency programs will not take any US exams into consideration for the Canadian match. It is therefore vital for Canadians studying in the US or elsewhere to obtain strong letters of recommendation to maximize their success for the Canadian residency match.

Experiential pearl:

I obtained letters of recommendations starting in my third clinical year of medical school. After each rotation has ended, I would ask for a letter of recommendation from my primary attending. Sometimes, I would ask for a letter from each of the attendings I had worked with.

I always provided an envelop with the address labelled and postage already paid, I also included a piece of paper folded inside the envelop with the procedure needed for a letter of recommendation that was provided by my school. I was able to obtain twelve letters of recommendations from both US attendings and Canadian attendings that I had worked with. This was more than enough to apply to residency. I managed to obtain letters of recommendation in specialties including OBGYN, family medicine, psychiatry, internal medicine, which was more than enough for application to primary care residencies in the US and Canada.

During my two months of rotations in Canada, I managed to obtain two letters of recommendation from Canadian family physicians, and three letters of recommendation from clinical professors or internal medicine at the University of Toronto.

*"When you walk up to opportunities door, don't knock it... Kick that b*tch in, smile and introduce yourself."*
- Dwaye "The Rock" Johnson

Section 14:
The minimalist guide to writing personal statements for CaRMS/ERAS

The personal statement is arguably one of the most important pieces in the application. This warrants some discussion. One must be cognizant of the fact that during the residency application process, in the US or Canada, when there can literally be thousands of applications going through a single residency program, a good to-the-point, easy-to-read personal statement could be the difference between getting an interview, OR having your entire application thrown into the trash.

During my interview process in the US, I have been told by some interviewers that the personal statement I wrote was excellent, and should be a textbook example of how a personal statement should be written. See what I wrote, see what I did, and learn from it.

In all US applications, you should answer the following three questions: **1) Why you chose the specialty you are applying to. 2) Why you would prefer to go to a specific program as opposed to the countless other programs available** (be as honest as you can! "I just want to match into a program is not a good answer!). **3) What would make you a good candidate compared to the countless others?**

Wherever possible, elaborate on life experiences that solidified your choice for a particular specialty.

There are many websites and books who discuss in great detail about the process of writing a great personal statement. I have provided the exact personal statements that I used for my applications, including the prompt questions for all the Canadian medical schools that I applied to. Out of the eight Canadian medical schools that I applied to (University of Toronto, Ottawa University, McMaster University, Northern Ontario School of Medicine, Queen's University, University of Western Ontario, McGill, University of British Columbia), I received invitations for interview from seven of them, with the exception the University of British Columbia.

I have included my complete Canadian residency application personal statements at the end of the book, under the **appendix section**.

Interviewer: *"tell me a joke"*

Candidate: *"uh... how much does a polar bear weigh? ... Enough to break the ice... Oh wait, that's a pickup line..."*
Interviewer: *"that is also acceptable"*

- *overheard on the interview trail 2014*

Section 15:
Strategies for interviews

Congrats! You have passed all your pre-clinical years, all your shelf exams, and now you are applying to residency programs. Now is time to prepare!

How to maximize interview invites in the US:

Pennsylvania is a very international friendly state. Out of the ten or so programs in FM that I applied for in Pennsylvania, I was invited to interview at nine of them. All of the programs I interviewed at also happened to be H1B granting. This is in contrast to ultra competitive states like California, where I applied to slightly more than twenty programs, but only interviewed at three sites.

Program directors will at times determine who to invite to their program for an interview based on geography - for example, if you live in far away California, and you are applying to a community program in rural Arkansas, from the program director's perspective, what are the odds that their program will attract someone from California to fly all the way to

Arkansas, and to rank that program as their top choice? A lot of program directors will choose candidates based on their geological proximity to the program site because their job is to make sure that all spots in their residency will be filled with residents come match day. For example, if you spent a lot of time in New York State, or have strong family ties to New York state, perhaps you will have a better chance of being invited to a program in New Jersey, simply because you had connections to locations close to New Jersey.

Similarly, if you went to school on the West coast and are applying to programs on the Eastern seaboard, program directors or those in charge of selection for interviews and ranking might be more reluctant to offer an interview simply because you come from a location that is very far away, and the likelihood of your accepting an invitation to interview, or the likelihood of your ranking that program high is lower than another candidate who comes from a closer geographical location.

Experiential pearl:

Some people might be tempted to apply only to states around the oceans (e.g. Florida, California) for the lifestyle that they perceive they will have. I would not recommend doing this. The issue is that American graduates (who naturally have an easier time with residency matching) will also be tempted to apply to these popular locations. What ends up happening is that the Canadian applicant, or any applicant needing a visa will have an extremely difficult time getting interviews in these popular spots.

Furthermore, more renowned US residency programs may offer the coveted H1B work visa for

Canadians graduating from American medical schools, but not for Canadians who are IMGs. I have come across several examples where family medicine programs at famous places such as the Mayo Clinic, Georgetown University offered me the H1B work visa if I matched. Their program website was also very clear that the H1B can only be offered to foreigners who are AMGs, but not IMGs.

What to do if you don't get enough interview invites:

If one does not receive enough interviews, or has not heard back from one of their top choices, then they can simply email or call to ask if the application has been received. Time permitting, one can simply state that they are passing through the area, and that they are interested in the program and would love to attend an interview. Simply by expressing interest and following up, one can likely obtain a few extra interviews.

How to determine whether a US program is DO friendly:

One strategy is to have a look on their website to see how many DOs are in their intern, PGY2, PGY3 classes. If there are no DOs at all in any of their years, you can assume that the location is not DO friendly.

Experiential pearl:

I actually applied to places that sponsored the H1B and had no DOs in any of their prior year classes, I still got interviews. Maybe it was because for US applicants, visa wasn't a problem, and no DOs applied there because of the program's reputation for being IMG/MD heavy.

I have had quite a few experiences in which I applied to IMG/MD heavy programs, and was still invited for interview.

US interview expectations of a Canadian AMG versus an US AMG:

As a Canadian AMG (either DO or MD), my experience is that you will not receive as many invites as your US AMG colleagues. However, you will most likely receive much more invitations that the IMGs who are foreign citizens.

I would say I was receiving at least twice as many interview invites as a foreign IMG applying to the same spots (who have higher board scores than me), and I only applied to half to 1/3 of the number of spots IMGs applied to. I ended up going to more interviews than most of the US AMGs simply because they can afford to cancel on interview invites. But I accepted all my invitations, so even though I received fewer invitations, I ended up going to more interviews than the US AMGs.

US interview expectations of a Canadian AMG versus a Canadian IMG:

What I have seen is that a lot of Canadian IMGs with much higher USMLE step 1 and step 2 board scores than me simply were not getting nearly as many interview invitations as me. It really is that bad. I have seen, and have been told by Canadian IMGs that people scoring in the 240s-250s on the USMLE step 1, and who are applying to Family Medicine in the US (the easiest specialty to match), are getting maybe 2 interviews, sometimes no interviews!

And for those Canadian IMGs getting decent number of interviews, they usually applied to 100 to 150 spots in family medicine, and received perhaps 7-9 interviews. As a DO, I applied to 49 programs in the US, and received 15 interviews.

Experiential pearl:

The brutal truth is, as AMGs, regardless of whether you are a MD or a DO, you are in a much better position in terms of receiving invitations for interviews than IMGs. Not getting interviews, or getting dangerously low numbers of interviews really is a theme for Canadian IMGs. I have met many IMGs on the interview trail; I can only say that their faces looked very sad.

On the interview trail, I once accidentally made a French Canadian girl cry... Don't ask an IMG how many interview invites they have. Chances are, they applied to 130-150, even 200 programs, and only got 6-7 interviews. Then she asked me how many invites I got. I easily tripled her interview number, and applied to a third as many spots as she did. Then she started rubbing her eyes and tearing up. She said she was "crying inside". Then she cussed at how bad it was for IMGs, especially foreign ones.

Experiential pearl:

I have scoured the internet forums regarding the interview process, and I have easily met hundreds of interviewees on the interview trail. The brutal truth that I have come to realize is that (foreign) IMGs ask: **"Will I match?" while USDOs ask: "where will I match"?**

There is an unspoken, natural pecking order for the match in the US. Needless to say, US trained MDs (especially US citizens or permanent residents) get the first pick. I have visited residency programs where the residency coordinator told me that they have not received a single application from a US trained MD in over twenty years. Why is this? Location, location, location! These programs tend to be located in relatively run-down towns with massive layoffs, or an industry (such as mining, steel, or hard industry) went bankrupt and left behind a broken community with relatively high rates of poverty and other social ills. The type of people who tend to match into these places are scramblers (i.e., they didn't match anywhere of their choice, and had to take the spot here, or not match at all), or sometimes legitimate US trained MDs who grew up in that place, and they truly want to return to the communities to help however they can. These places also tend to be heavy in IMGs, especially foreign IMGs in need of visa, as US trained MDs tend to have better options at their disposal.

How many interviews should I attend? How many programs should I rank?

It is very important to review the **ACGME match data** compiled by the **national resident matching program (NRMP)**. Starting in 2016, the NRMP started compiling data for US osteopathic graduates. What is interesting to see is the number of contiguous ranks versus the probability of match for each specialty.

Google search **"Charting Outcomes in the Match for U.S. Osteopathic Medical Students and Graduates"**. It has graphical representation of the number of programs that an applicant ranks contiguously (in total) versus the probability of their matching into a program (based on specialty). There are similar graphs with different curves for each discipline.

Take the graph for **family medicine** for example, on **page 46** of this document. For a US trained DO, if you interviewed and ranked 15 programs, your chance of matching into a residency of family medicine would approach 100% (1). If you applied to only one program, then your chance of matching is about 60% (1). If you wish to apply to other specialties besides family medicine, study NRMP publication carefully, it contains similar graphs for all other specialties.

Similar statistics can be found if you are a **US MD** candidate in the ACGME match. The NRMP publication you should be looking for is **"Charting Outcomes in the Match for U.S. Allopathic Seniors"**. Take the graph for family medicine yet again, on **page 66** of this document. As a US MD who applied to family medicine, once you ranked 13 programs contiguously, your chance of acceptance into a program approaches 100% (2). If you applied to only one program, then your chance of matching is almost 80% (2), 20% higher than your US DO colleague.

For family medicine, a safe cut-off is between 13 to 15 programs to ensure an almost 100% chance of a successful match. This is the reason why I would recommend all US MDs and US DOs to apply to around 50 programs, which should result interview invites for around 15-20 programs. A safe number is to interview at 15 US spots, then rank at least 13 - 15 ACGME programs to maximize their chance of matching (somewhere) in the US.

As an **IMG candidate** to the ACGME match, look for the NRMP publication **"Charting Outcomes in the Match for International Medical Graduates".** The process becomes much more difficult as can be seen from the same example for family medicine. Turn to **page 86**. As an IMG without US citizenship, one would need to rank 20 ACGME programs in order to get a ~60% chance for a successful match at a family medicine program (3).

References:

(1) Charting Outcomes in the Match for U.S. Osteopathic Medical Students and Graduates

http://www.nrmp.org/wp-content/uploads/2016/09/Charting-Outcomes-US-Osteopathic-2016.pdf

Accessed January 24th, 2017.

(2) Charting Outcomes in the Match for U.S. Allopathic Seniors

http://www.nrmp.org/wp-content/uploads/2016/09/Charting-Outcomes-US-Allopathic-Seniors-2016.pdf

Accessed January 24th, 2017

(3) Charting Outcomes in the Match for International Medical Graduates

http://www.nrmp.org/wp-content/uploads/2016/09/Charting-Outcomes-IMGs-2016.pdf

Accessed January 24th, 2017

How to prepare for interviews:

For family medicine, the types of questions asked on interviews are designed to assess the type of person you are, and how well you would fit into a residency program. The people asking the questions basically just want to get to know you.

For specialist programs, the interview questions tend to be more difficult, often leaning on testing your medical knowledge. One can be asked questions regarding medicine and medical management.

Unfortunately, one needs to have a good foundation in medical knowledge to do well these types of interviews.

A good general resource is the University of Washington, Department of Family Medicine's residency interview page:

https://depts.washington.edu/fammed/education/advising/apply/interview-preparing-yourself/

It has a good list of questions, and suggestions for preparing for your interview. What I did was I obtained that list of questions on their website, and wrote out script-like answers to all the questions. Then I memorized the key points of my answers, and rehearsed all of them. This way, you will have a defined set of answers to the most common questions.

Tips for scheduling interviews and elective rotations:

This point is especially relevant if you are a **US MD who has Canadian interviews, or an IMG/ US DO with interviews in Quebec.** Canada has interviews set for the end of January and early February of each year. When setting up your rotations for 4th year, try to keep 2 to 4 weeks empty between the middle to end of January through early February so you can fill in Canadian interview dates for that time slot. This point is vital as all Canadian programs will interview during that 4 week period, and they only have interview days on 2 maybe 5 days of the year during that time.

If is vital to get time off during this period in order to attend these Canadian interviews. If you are obligated to do clinical rotations during that same period, and **you are unable to get any days off**

rotation, then unfortunately, you will be unable to come to the Canadian interview.

See **MLK day** for details for strategies.

It is different for CMGs in that Canadian schools know that CaRMS interview season is around that time, so CMGs usually have those 3 to 4 weeks off to travel the country for interviews. For US medical students or IMGs/CSAs/USDOs, we don't have this luxury, and we really need to schedule this vital time between the end of January and beginning of February diligently.

Experiential pearl:

My experience still applies to Canadians at US MD schools, and US DOs attempting the CaRMS match in Quebec.

The good news is that CaRMS publishes the dates for the specialties of choice pretty early in the application process, almost 6 months in advance of interview day. You can go on the CaRMS website, and look up the scheduled interview days, then make a preliminary interview schedule by assuming which institution invitations you will receive. CaRMS interview schedules can be found here:

http://www.CaRMS.ca/en/residency/r-1/interview-schedule/

I did exactly this, and I was able to figure out a schedule to attend every family medicine program that I was invited to. Then I scheduled my US rotations based on the CaRMS interview schedule. Even so, I had four CaRMS interviews in the middle of one of my US rotations, and I was able to solve this problem by putting them into the **MLK week** (see for details).

The difference between American and Canadian interviews:

The US interviews typically have around 20 or more interview dates spread over a few months (around late October, through end of January). Each interview day can have as high as ten candidates in attendance, and as low as one or two candidates for that particular day. I have experienced both extremes. Almost all US interviews will have a face to face interview with the program director. This I find is unique to the US system. There are also no weekend interviews in the US. Of all the US interviews I have done, and everyone I have talked to, I have not come across interviews on weekends.

The Canadian system is quite different. Instead of having 20 or more interview days spread over 3 months, Canadian interviews (for all specialties!) occur over the course of 3-4 weeks. Each specialty in each university (for example, family medicine at McMaster University) will only have 2-7 scheduled interview days during the 3-4 week interview window. Each interview day can have two sessions - one in the morning, and one in the afternoon. Each session can have as much as 100 or more applicants present for the interview. A big difference is that with such large numbers, applicants in Canada will rarely if ever have one on one interview time with the program director. This is the case for programs with lots of positions like family medicine. In specialties with much smaller number of seats, like radiation oncology, this probably will not be the case. Another interesting point is that some Canadian programs will conduct weekend interviews. This can be an important way for applicants to make it for these interviews if weekdays were not an option.

Experiential pearl:

Keep checking the CaRMS website, as unlike the US system in which interview dates are given **after** you are invited for interview. The Canadian system works such that interview dates are pre-determined even before all the invitations are mailed out. What this means is that you can figure out your interview schedule (while making the assumption that the programs you applied to will actually invite you) several months in advance of the actual invitations.

When I applied to CaRMS and was scheduling my 4th year rotations in the US, I did not know this vital piece of information. I didn't realize that Canadian interview dates were published well before the actual invitation to interview.

I managed to schedule enough time between the end of one rotation and the start of the next to successfully book and attend **seven** Canadian interviews.

Martin Luther King (MLK) day:

MLK day is a statutory holiday in the US, and will be very helpful during your CaRMS interviews. This holiday falls on January 20th. This time is vital for US students, especially when they ask for multiple days off during rotations in the US. You can potentially ask for the entire week of Jan 20th (assuming it's a Monday) off for Canadian interviews, then come back to the US the next week to continue your rotation. My school allowed 3 weekdays off per 4 week rotation for purposes of interviews. I had MLK day off (a Monday), then I asked for the next 3 days of the week (Tuesday, Wednesday, Thursday) off, and I also got Friday off by coming in an extra day on another weekend to make up for Friday. I was able to schedule the entire week off, and still finish the US rotation on time, without falling out of track for my last year of medical school.

The reason I had to do this was because I had four of my Canadian interviews fall right in the third week of this four week rotation. Lucky for me, I scheduled these four interviews in the week of MLK day. With MLK day being a Monday, and a holiday that is not celebrated in Canada, I was able to attend all 4 Canadian interviews. This would not have been possible had it not been a MLK day week.

US interviews typically occur starting the middle of October, and go all the way to February of the next year. I would recommend that you get all your US interviews out of the way first before starting your Canadian interviews. Similarly, for the US, you might want to leave a 2 week empty spot between mid November to mid December to schedule the US interviews.

I managed to take a two week break early November, and packed in nine interviews across five Eastern states in two weeks (15 whole days, 10 business days). **I drove 2853 miles, averaging 190 miles a day.** I crossed five US states from Ohio to New York to interview at these sites.

Hopefully you'll have applied to enough programs, and invited to enough programs that you can pack in all these interviews back to back, nonstop. That is the most efficient way to go about US interviews.

Some people hate interview season, because you have to think fast, and be quick about your scheduling. The moment you flinch, a good interview date could be taken by someone else. I was very successful on the interview trail, and quite frankly, I rather enjoyed the whole experience.

Interview etiquette:

In the US, it is customary to write "**thank you notes**", or at least sent a "thank you email" after having an interview in that program. Send notes to all people who interviewed you. Do not forget to also send a note to the program coordinator - as they are the ones who schedule the interviews, and make the interviews possible. They are the people often forgotten during "thank you note" time, but now you know better!

Second looks:

These are designed purely to help you gauge how "right" a program is for you. You'll probably spent half a day following a resident team in their service to see what gets done. Most programs will say that "second looks" are for the applicant only, and does not affect how the program will rank the applicant.

However, **if** you are an IMG, and you only had two to four interviews, perhaps you should go for a second look at your few programs, just to get your face seen, and to around during ranking time.

The funds needed for interview season:

I would recommend preparing **10,000 US dollars** in preparation for your interviews in the US and Canada. Being invited to interviews is an honour; I would go to as many of them as possible. You should be grateful that you can spend the money to go to these interviews, compared to IMG applicants who don't get nearly enough invitations and can't go to these places even if they wanted to.

Word of caution on California and British Columbia

There are a few places in North America where the odds are stacked against you if you did not train at a certain institute, or you do not possess a piece of governmental document, or you are not a resident of a certain geographical area.

California is such a place. Having spent four years of medical school in California, it is apparent that this is a wonderful place. I can understand why everybody wants to come here. The stats (i.e., board scores, class ranking, etc) needed to be invited for an interview and for a successful match are probably the highest in the US. Americans from cooler climates are all lined up and clamouring to match into California. The same stats that will get you interviews on the East coast might not get you interviews in California. Because they receive so many applications, California is not friendly to foreign citizens (IMG or AMG) in need of visas at all. If a program in California is visa sponsoring, it is mostly the J1 visa, and not the H1B.

Experiential pearl:

Out of the 49 programs I applied to in the US, 19 were for California. I only ended up getting two interviews in California. This was when I understood that something else was going on that was not strictly based on board scores and hard stats. I have been invited to very famous programs in the US, including more than one Mayo Clinic, Georgetown in Washington DC, Cleveland Clinic. So I know my stats were good enough for well known programs. Geography wasn't an issue as I lived around Los Angeles, and could have easily driven to the dozen or so programs all around me within two hours. What I started noticing was that my classmates in California who had much lower step 1 scores than me, who had repeated a year of med school all ended up getting more interview invitations in California than I did. This made me conclude that there was a true bias against people in need of visas in California. It certainly felt like you get selected out of California programs because you needed a visa.

Expectations of British Columbia resident and coming back to UBC for residency:

UBC has a reputation for favouring graduates of their own program during the match, even when the competition is amongst CMGs. That is to say, if you are a graduate of UBC, then you have a higher chance of matching into GME at UBC vis-à-vis a CMG from another Canadian institution. You can imagine, if that is the case for CMGs between UBC and other Canadian med schools, the dichotomy between UBC grads and US MDs will be quite significant as well.

Experiential pearl:

Out of the eight family medicine programs I applied to in Canada, UBC was the only school that refused to give me an interview. I even received invitations to schools like NOSM (where you need substantial "ties" to Northern Ontario in order to have a decent match there), and also McGill - the only English institution in Quebec.

If you are an IMG graduate of an Irish school, you probably have a higher chance of matching into UBC than a US trained DO. I have heard of first hand experiences in which US trained DO candidates with two months of elective rotations at UBC failed to receive any interview invitations. I have also heard that Vancouver General Hospital is filled with IMGs from

Ireland, and the upper floors of that hospital has an Irish accent.

My advice to BC residents who attend US MD or US DO schools and who have their heart set on returning to UBC for graduate medical education is this: **don't hold your breath**. Unfortunately, it is highly unlikely at the present time for a US trained MD or DO to match back to UBC. The more viable option is to match on the East coast, namely, Ontario (for the US MD), maybe even Quebec (for the US MD or DO). After residency training, try to licensure in BC.

At the present moment a large portion of US trained DOs certified to practice medicine in Canada has set up shop in BC. So it seems that doing one's residency training is hard in BC, but after graduation, you can set up shop in BC without any difficulty.

A word on professionalism:

It is pretty hard to fail out of medical school. People who are asked to leave usually had a problem to do with **professionalism**.

Maybe you were divorced recently, maybe you broke up with your boyfriend or girlfriend, maybe your dog died, maybe you just had a thirty hour shift and you just want to go home and sleep, maybe you fell asleep on the wheels and almost got yourself killed on the drive home, maybe your ex wife recently got engaged and you are stuck doing scut work at your rotation.

Regardless of the circumstances, it is always important to keep a clear and cool head, and to think things through before acting on them.

Keep a **clean online profile**, especially Facebook. Online media is extremely important; you never know what the other person looking at your online personality across the computer screen might do.

It is also generally a good idea to keep your online identity as tidy as possible, so this means you should remove pictures of yourself in compromising situations (e.g., drunken pictures, inappropriate hand gestures, smoking weed, and visiting strip clubs).

Since you are in the medical profession now, you must always be cognizant of the fact that you will be watched closely by the public for the rest of your life. Especially in this day and age where screenshots, pictures, video can be easily recorded and distributed on the internet, one must always keep a well mannered online profile.

"The greatest pleasure in life is doing what people say you cannot do."

-Walter Bagehot quotes

Section 16:
Strategies for the US match

Timing of the match, AOA, vs. ACGME, vs. CaRMS:

The AOA match happens the earliest, in the middle of February. The CaRMS match happens second, in early March. The ACGME match happens last, in mid to late March. What this means is that if you match with the earlier organization, you are automatically pulled out of the later matches.

For example, if you applied to internal medicine with all 3 organizations: AOA, CaRMS, and ACGME. You would have a very real chance of matching FIRST into the AOA side (it really isn't that hard), once you match, you are pulled out of the CaRMS and ACGME match.

If your goal is to return to Canada, then matching the AOA really is NOT an option as you WILL probably match on the AOA side, and be pulled out of the Canadian side. If you want to have a reasonable chance of coming home to Canada and backing up with US programs, then ONLY apply to CaRMS and ACGME (bypass AOA).

Should I do the AOA match?

If your goal is primary care – family medicine, paediatrics, psychiatry, then it really isn't that hard to match into an ACGME residency program as a US trained DO, even if you are a Canadian in need of visa sponsorship. In this case, I would recommend matching to strictly ACGME programs, or at most, dually accredited AOA-ACGME programs- but apply through the ACGME side.

You would consider applying to the AOA side (of a strictly AOA-only program or a dually accredited AOA-ACGME program) if you have found AOA visa sponsoring specialties that are hard to match into as a DO in the ACGME world - perhaps dermatology, orthopaedics, anaesthesiology, etc.

It works like this: Let's assume you wanted to do emergency medicine, you have found a dually accredited AOA-ACGME program that was willing to give you the H1B visa in the US. You are unsure whether you will match into EM in Canada. You don't mind staying in the US to train in EM. And the only thing you want to do is emergency medicine. Well, you are in luck. To maximize your chances of success in this situation, you could apply to the AOA-side of a dually accredited AOA-ACGME program in EM. You have a higher chance of matching into EM in this case because you will be competing with a much smaller pool of DO applicants on the AOA-side of a dual program. You will not be competing in the much larger ACGME side of the match.

Experiential pearl:

I applied to several AOA-ACGME programs in family medicine in the US. I decided not to go through the AOA side, even though it increased your chance of matching in the US. I wanted to have a chance to match back in Canada. If I matched through the AOA, I would have effectively given up my chance for Canada. For primary care, it isn't hard at all to match into AOA programs.

What about OMM?! - A word of advice for DO applicants during the match:

OMM will always be a part of your professional title as an osteopathic physician. People with enough knowledge will ask you about OMM, residencies (in the US) will assume you know OMM. If you match back home in Canada, the provincial colleges might even invite you to give a talk about OMM!

If you match in the US as a DO in a dually accredited residency program, you will be trained like a DO even if you matched through the ACGME side. Some dually accredited programs will make it mandatory for you to take both the DO and MD specialty board exams as a way for them to maintain their dually accredited status.

If you match into a solely ACGME accredited program, then it is usually the case that these programs will not make any mandatory requirements that you practice your OMM, or take both sets of specialty boards.

Experiential pearl:

I have come across many dually accredited AOA - ACGME FM programs that made it perfectly clear that if I were to match into the program, regardless of the fact that I only matched through the ACGME side, and not the AOA side - that I was expected to write both sets of FM board exams - MD and DO. Also, even though I was applying to the ACGME side of a dual program, if I matched there, I was expected to train with the AOA curriculum (since I was a DO), regardless of the fact that I only applied to the ACGME side.

The point is, if you are a DO who ended up matching or practicing in the US, OMM will stay with you for a very long time, probably throughout your entire career. You see, if you are licensed through the AOA, you will need to keep your knowledge of OMM, especially for their recertification exams. OMM will also pop up in the CME credits. So it helps to have a general appreciation of OMM, and at least be functional in this treatment modality for the sake of your career.

OMM skills, DO graduates, and PM&R residency:

It is common knowledge that in the US, osteopathic graduates are sought after by PM&R residencies. This is due to the OMM training of osteopathic medical schools. DO students in general have a much more developed sense of tactile sensation via their hands compared to their MD counterparts.

Musculoskeletal medicine and training is also very stronger in a DO curriculum owing to the 200-400 hours of OMM training throughout a DO's medical education. The musculoskeletal background of a DO will come in handy during PM&R residency training, and it is fairly common for the DO to match into ACGME PM&R programs with these aforementioned qualities.

Even in the medical student level, most attendings will comment that DO students tend to be more comfortable with physical touch, and manual palpation of musculoskeletal systems when it comes to patient care, something that their MD counterparts have a much harder time with simply because OMM isn't a part of their training.

The US match as an AMG versus an IMG:

In 2016, the **success rate of US DOs in the US ACGME match was 80.3%**, while that of **US MDs was 93.8%** (1). As a Canadian attending either a US MD or DO school, your ACGME match rate will fall into either of those two categories mentioned (i.e., either 80.3% for USDO (excluding the AOA match) and 93.8% for USMD).

The 2016 AMG match rate in CaRMs was 54.5% (2). So if you compared the ACGME match with the Canadian match for 2016, you can see that for AMGs, **the US numbers are much higher than the CaRMS numbers (i.e., 80.3% and 93.8% versus 54.5%)** (2).

The success rate of IMGs (i.e., non-US citizens such as Canadian CSAs/IMGs) on the US ACGME match is much lower compared to the AMG match at 50.5% (1). **The success rate is even lower for Canadian CSAs/IMGs in the Canadian match at only 22.0%** (2). But a 50.5% success rate is still more than double the Canadian IMG match rate of 22.0%.

Keep in mind that the cost of American and international medical training can easily go into the three hundred thousand dollars range. The absolute worst thing that can happen is to graduate medical school without securing a residency spot.

With the CaRMS match numbers for AMGs and IMGs in mind, **I would argue that for Canadians attending medical school outside of Canada, regardless of whether you are in the US or in an international school, you should first and foremost plan to match into an US ACGME program.**

For further discussion regarding the US match and Canadian match, please refer to figure 2, section 6 - **Why should I choose an American DO or MD medical school over an international school?**

Bottom line:

Simply put, there is a higher success rate in the US ACGME match for both Canadian AMGs and IMGs. Therefore, for Canadians studying medicine outside of Canada, they should aim for an ACGME match.

References:

(1) National Residency Matching Program- Results and Data, 2016 Main Residency Match. Washington DC. 2016 Available at:
http://www.nrmp.org/wp-content/uploads/2016/04/Main-Match-Results-and-Data-2016.pdf

(2) Canadian Resident Matching Service (CaRMS). Reports & Statistics - R-1 Match Reports - 2016. Ottawa, ON: Canadian Resident Matching Service; 2016. Available at:
http://www.carms.ca/wp-content/uploads/2016/05/Table_1_Summary_of_Match_Results_English.pdf

"It is possible to commit no mistakes and still lose. That is not weakness. That is life."

-Captain Jean Luc Picard, Star trek TNG

Section 17: Strategies for the Canadian match

How will recent CaRMS changes affect USDOs in the Canadian match?

Starting in 2017, all USDOs will be considered IMGs for the CaRMS match (except Quebec). Many people were concerned with this new change and their chances of coming back home to Canada. Looking at prior CaRMS match success rates for USDOs, there were at most one to three matches made in CaRMS a year. Most Canadians didn't bother to come back, and those who did have to do a lot more work to get back.

The majority of matches were for family medicine, and there were only one to three successful matches each year. So as a Canadian going to a USDO school, your chance of coming back to Canada for residency wasn't too high to begin with, your best shot was always to have matched with the ACGME in the US. The recent changes for CaRMS aren't too devastating if you look at it from this perspective.

No one ever said that by going to a USDO school (or even a US MD school), one would have a good chance of matching back to Canada for residency. It has always been advised that the best bet was to stay in the US for residency, then attempt to come back to Canada to practice after US residency training.

Even if you had first iteration CaRMS rights in Ontario as a USDO, it wasn't a guarantee that you would match. I have seen Canadian DOs go on five CaRMS interviews and not match into a single program. Nothing is guaranteed when it comes to the CaRMS match. One's best chance of practicing in Canada as a USDO graduate was and will continue to be completion of US residency training, then attempt to return home after US residency training.

CaRMS match as an American medical graduate (AMG):

Generally, it is **"difficult"** to match in Canada even as an AMG. For the 2016 CaRMS match, only 18 out of 33 **(54.5%)** of AMGs (i.e. USMDs) matched via CaRMS (1). With these numbers, it seems that even attending a USMD school will not translate into a high chance of matching back into Canada for residency, as only one out of two AMG candidates made it back to Canada in 2016.

CaRMS match as an international medical graduate (IMG):

For IMG candidates, in my opinion, the numbers can only be described as being "abysmal" at a 22.0% match rate in 2016, where only 408 of 1815 candidates managed to obtain a Canadian residency spot (1).

In comparison, the 2016 US ACGME match rate for IMGs was 54.5% (2). In both cases, both Canadian AMGs and IMGs have a higher rate of success matching into US ACGME programs. With the Canadian match being what it is, **I would argue that the best strategy is to focus one's energies on the US ACGME match, and attempt the CaRMS match only if one is really adamant about doing residency in Canada.**

References:

(1) Canadian Resident Matching Service (CaRMS). R-1 Match Reports – 2016. Ottawa, ON: Canadian Resident Matching Service; 2016. Available at: http://www.carms.ca/wp-content/uploads/2016/05/Table_1_Summary_of_Match_Results_English.pdf

(2) National Residency Matching Program. 2016 Main Residency Match. Washington, DC: 2016. Available at: http://www.nrmp.org/wp-content/uploads/2016/04/Main-Match-Results-and-Data-2016.pdf

The IMG competition pool in Canada:

Interviewing as an IMG for family medicine in Ontario is unique in that there is only one interview for (potentially) all six universities in Ontario. The interview site is located in Toronto, and the IMG is expected to sit on a panel style interview for the Universities that grant them an interview. For example, if the IMG applied for family medicine in Ontario, and was granted interviews in three of the six universities - then the panel would consist of representatives from the three universities.

I have been told that the type of competition one would meet in the first iteration IMG match usually consists of forty to fifty year olds, with medical degrees and residency training from other countries. These people tend to be new immigrants to Canada, and simply want to obtain a job and secure their livelihoods in a new country. I have also been told that younger Canadian born graduates of international medical schools tend to have a better match rate than these middle aged IMG immigrants simply for the reason that they have a better command of the English language and is more in-tune with Canadian culture.

Tips for the US MD in the Canadian match:

Having a US MD will not automatically mean that you are given the golden key to residency in Canada. Even if you are a US MD, if you have not done your due diligence, if you have not done an adequate amount of electives in your specialty of choice in Canada, if you have no Canadian letters of recommendation, and you applied to CaRMS, you will probably not receive any interviews.

I saw this exact scenario unfold. I met a Canadian citizen on the interview trail in the US who was a US MD graduate, he applied to IM and FM for CaRMS, and did not receive a single Canadian interview (even though he in theory had the first iteration in all Canadian provinces, and for all practical purposes, should have been considered on the same footing as a CMG). Unfortunately, he did not do any Canadian electives at all, and stayed in America his entire four years. As such, he received no Canadian invites.

Word of caution on UBC:

Although UBC technically allows Canadians at American medical schools (US MD) first iteration CMG stream access to their CaRMS match, the reality is quite different. For Canadians of US MD schools, we are only aware of one Canadian who attended a US MD school who managed to match into UBC within the last five years. UBC is one of the most competitive institutions in Canada. Their residency spots usually go filled in the first iteration for CMGs, and it is an extremely competitive institution.

Experiential pearl:

The strategy to maximize your chances for an UBC interview and to minimize the cost of application is to **not** apply to all discipline specific program sites at once.

For example, the family medicine residency program at UBC consists of around twelve different sites (locations spread far apart). The cost of application to each site is approximately 30 dollars Canadian. Applying to all family medicine training sites at UBC would cost slightly over three hundred dollars Canadian. Chances are, owing to the competitiveness of all UBC spots, an AMG likely will not receive an invitation to interview at UBC. Instead, apply to one or two large program sites at UBC, and wait for an interview invitation (if any). In Canada, a candidate is invited to a single interview for all residency program sites (in the discipline) that they applied to. They can even add additional discipline specific program sites after completing their interview, and still be considered at those added sites post interview.

It would be a mistake to apply to all of the family medicine program sites at UBC, then to wait for an interview. Chances are that for AMGs, we most likely will not receive any interviews, and we would have effectively lost ~300 dollars. Instead, apply to only one of their program sites. If you get invited for interview, you can always pay the fee to add the other sites later -

this is a practical way to save money and maximize your application!

Section 18:
US visa fundamentals

Visas revisited (relevant to US MDs, US DOs, CSAs/IMGs):
There are two potential types of visas.

1) H1B visa: This is the harder visa to get from US immigration. It allows you to stay in the US after your training, and puts you on the path to getting a green card, which can eventually lead to the option of getting US citizenship.

Unfortunately, this visa costs the program money to obtain. Most competitive specialties will not offer an H1B visa, because they have more than enough applications from qualified US applicants, and the few foreign applicants that they get would be more than happy to settle for a J-1 visa.

Non-competitive specialties in the US like family medicine, paediatrics, psychiatry, etc, often offer H1B visas to their foreign applicants as an incentive in order to fill their programs and avoid going unfilled.

Additionally, if you were a CMG or IMG who did not graduate from a US medical school, then you cannot apply for this visa unless you have taken and passed

USMLE Step 3. You cannot take the USMLE Step 3 until after you graduate medical school. You then need to take and pass this exam, and get the results before you can start applying for the H1B visa. That means for IMGs and CMGs who are starting a US residency, it is extremely hard to graduate from medical school and start internship/residency on time on July 1.

But, if you were an AMG and was a graduate of a US MD or DO school, then this rule does not apply to you. Foreign citizens of a US MD or DO schools are not required to complete the USMLE or COMLEX in order to obtain H1B visa sponsorship.

The USMLE step 3 and the H1B visa

We used to think that as AMGs (both MD and DO), we'd also need to pass the USMLE step 3 in order to receive the coveted H1B visa. However, this is not the case.

This website summarizes the requirements succinctly: **http://www.doctorsimmigrationlaw.com/work-visas/h-1b-options-for-doctors**

If you are an IMG, or a CMG (anyone who completed medical school outside the US), and you want the H1B visa, then you would need to complete the USMLE step 1, step 2 CK, step 2 CS, and step 3. However, if you are a foreign citizen but an AMG (such as a Canadian studying at a USMD, or USDO medical school (both would be considered AMGs)), then the rule of completing the USMLEs steps 1, 2 and 3 for the H1B does not apply.

Specifically as a USDO, you are also not required to have completed the USMLE series for the H1B visa, as the completed COMLEX series will suffice.

What this means is that you don't have to rush to have your USMLE step 3 (as a USMD), or COMLEX part 3 (as a USDO) completed before residency starts in order to obtain the H1B visa! Whereas for IMGs, they would need to complete the USMLE step 3 right after fourth year of medical school before they can receive their H1B visa.

Experiential pearls:

I had initially signed up for the USMLE step 2 CS under the mistaken impression that I needed the complete USMLEs to be eligible for the H1B visa. Non-US citizen IMGs who matched into US residency programs always had to complete the USMLE series to be eligible for the H1B visa, and I had simply assumed that the complete USMLEs was needed for American medical graduates as well (US MD and US DO). No one was around to tell me otherwise. After doing further research, I had to figure it out the hard way that the USMLE series was not needed for H1B sponsorship for non-US citizens who are AMGs, and also that there is no refund for the USMLE step 2 CS (at a cost of US $~1200). I then cancelled my USMLE step 2 CS exam as passing the exam would offer no additional benefits for me, while failing the test could be devastating.

Furthermore, I had also come across a Canadian DO graduate doing psychiatry residency in California under the H1B, who only finished the COMLEX series, and stopped at the USMLE step 2 CK. If you want the J1 visa, then you'd need the step 2 CK, but not the step 2 CS.

2) J-1 visa: This is the more likely visa that you will end up with if you are applying to a competitive specialty, such as dermatology, plastic surgery, ophthalmology,

ENT, urology, radiology, etc. This visa is easier to obtain from your residency program. A catch is that you need **Health Canada** to issue you a "**Statement of Need (SON)**", which is a letter stating that Canada needs more physicians in your specialty. If you can't get this letter, you can't get a J-1 visa.

One should also be cognizant of the fact that Health Canada only issues so many SONs per specialty. For instance, for 2015, there is only four SONs for urology, which is given on a first come first serve basis. What this means is that for all Canadians studying medical school outside of Canada, who then desire to pursue an urology residency in the US under the J1 visa, only four such Canadians will be able to obtain the SON for urology from Health Canada.

For primary care specialties like family medicine, pediatrics, general internal medicine, psychiatry, getting the J1 visa would be no issue as Health Canada offers unlimited, or more SON endorsements than the demand. But the moment one is considering specialties and J1 visa, one must be extremely careful.

The other issue with the J-1 visa is that you need to come back to Canada for 2 years once your training is complete. If you don't want to do that, you can apply for a J-1 waiver in the US, which means that you will work in a VA (Veteran's Administration) hospital in the US for 3 years, or an underserved area of the US for 3 years. Both of these options can be distasteful for a number of reasons.

General information on J1 visa and Statement of Need:

http://www.hc-sc.gc.ca/hcs-sss/hhr-rhs/postgrad-postdoc/index-eng.php

Statement of Need quota:
http://www.hc-sc.gc.ca/hcs-sss/hhr-rhs/postgrad-postdoc/cat_b-list-liste-eng.php

The ideal J1 timeline and summary:

Early 3rd year

- Research and confirm with all applied programs that they offer J1 visa

April-May of M3

- Email all potential programs for Visa requirement. Don't rely entirely on Visa information through **FREIDA Online**. Email programs individually (program coordinator and program director)

Early 4th year

- Obtain ECFMG number to obtain access to OASIS to apply for DS-2019

March of 4th year

- Wait for results from match day
- Contact Health Canada Administrator for checklist of documents for statement of need
- Contact residency coordinator re: starting sponsorship process for J1
- Contact health force Ontario for advisor for action plan
- Collect letters and documents for health Canada packet

- Contact school to request for letter of intent (2 copies) for upcoming graduation to be mailed to Health Canada
- Upload documents into OASIS
- Make contact with the TPL of your program
- Once statement of need has been issued and all documents uploaded, wait for word on approval for DS-2019
- DS-2019 will be issued from ECFMG to your program and your program will be responsible for forwarding it to you
- Upon receiving DS-2019, pay SEVIS fee of $180

June before internship

- Bring DS2019 and necessary documents to US port of entry to enter via J1 status
- Bring passport, DS-2019, I-94 with D/S status to your program to confirm of your arrival
- After being in the US on J1 status for 10 days, can apply for social security number

Some Random Tips regarding J1 visa:

- Ideally, you'd want to rotate at places that sponsor visas. Do one round of verification for elective sites to make sure they offer visa **and** a second round of verification when you apply for residency.
- Do not solely rely on visa information from FREIDA online (some may claim they offer visa, but don't; while others may not state they offer visas, but they do!) contact the programs individually to double check.
- **Before** you schedule the interview, double check they offer the type of Visa you want! (Uninformed secretaries are hard to blame).

- Be very familiar with what you have to do for the visa before the match and prepare some documents early if possible. Please note that many letters cannot be done until after the match as they require the letter of offer or match screenshot from your residency.
- Request for a letter of intent for graduation from your school right after the match. This can take a while and needs to be sent to Health Canada. You can request your school to send it out and they can do so via FedEx. Make sure you stay on top of school to get this letter as this can become the limiting factor to obtaining your statement of need.
- You will also need a letter of intent for ECMFG to take place of the copy of your degree as you will be applying prior to graduation. Make sure your ECFMG number is included on this letter. You can ask for this one to be emailed as you can upload it into OASIS to take place of your medical school diploma.
- AOA accredited residencies are off the table if you want to return to Canada to practice.

How do I know if a program is visa sponsoring?

The starting point is to visit **FREIDA,** a free database of ACGME accredited residencies and fellowships.

One should check on FREIDA regularly to see if program is H1B sponsoring or not.
A lot of the time, programs will state that they do not give the H1B to IMGs, but will make exceptions and sponsor the H1B for foreign citizens who are AMGs. So make sure to email or call those programs, and explain the situation.

For example, if you were an IMG, you would only be eligible for the J1 visa. But if you were a foreign citizen who graduated from a US medical school (either

USMD or USDO), you are then an AMG, and in a lot of cases, they will sponsor the H1B visa for you.

For example, the Mayo Clinic (Rochester, Minnesota) is such an institution. IMG candidates are given the J1 visa, but any foreign citizen who is a graduate of a US medical school, regardless of DO or MD, will be eligible for the H1B visa.

Optional Practical Training Year (OPT)

As a foreign citizen and American medical graduate, you would have been on the F1 student visa during your four years of medical school in the US. Upon completion of medical school, you can transition into the **Optional Practical Training** year that is a part of your F1 visa. The OPT year lasts approximately one year, and can cover your visa status regardless of J1 or H1B sponsorship (via your residency program) for your first year of residency.

Is getting the H1B difficult?
AOA / ACGME programs:

Up until recently, It was thought that H1B visas are extremely hard to come by, and this type of visa was mostly given by ACGME (MD) programs. However, this line of thought is not entirely correct. There actually exists a very significant and large number of dually accredited AOA and ACGME residencies (especially in family medicine, and primary care) who will sponsor H1B visas.

Visit FREIDA:

If a program was dually accredited, it would show up on FREIDA. You would then need to visit the program website to confirm whether the H1B visa was granted in these programs. Better yet, call the program to ask and confirm their visa policy!

Experiential pearl:

I only applied to family medicine programs. I could have applied to psychiatry, or internal medicine, but I decided upon family medicine for a variety of reasons.

I received 15 US interviews, at really famous programs as well. 13 agreed to H1B sponsorship (these included dually AOA - ACGME accredited programs, as well as solely ACGME-accredited programs), and only 2 sites were strictly J1 sponsoring (which I ranked low for obvious reasons).

Experiential pearl:

You will try your best, but programs change all the time, so be prepared to head to interviews where you thought the program was H1B sponsoring, but in actuality, they cannot due to unforeseen events.

This situation happened to me on the interview trail. I was invited to an interview in Ohio. I researched their website, and it stated that they were H1B sponsoring. However, during the actual interview, I was told that the hospital has been purchased by another institution, and will be changed to for-profit status - meaning they will no longer sponsor the H1B visa. Their website was in fact out of date, as they were bought out very recently, and their website did not reflect this change. They offered me the J1 visa.

Don't feel too bad if this happens, and it is bound to happen if you have a large number of interviews. Simply cross that specific site off your ranking list (if you desire a specific visa), and move onto the next interview! This is also precisely another reason why you should buffer your US interviews with at least 10-15 interviews to cushion against unfortunate situations like this.

Section 19:
How to obtain state licensure in the United States

Definition of key terms:

Preliminary year - one year position in a given field (i.e. Internal Medicine or Surgery) usually preceding training in another specialty

Transitional year - one year position with rotations through various disciplines (e.g. Internal Medicine, Surgery, etc.); also precedes training in other specialties

Categorical position - first year in a program in which the applicant will remain for all of his/her residency training (cf. preliminary year)

State licensure:

If you want to practice medicine, then you will need a license to do it. Physician licensing is state-specific. As osteopathic medical students, you can't get a license unless you have graduated from an osteopathic medical school and successfully completed a certain number of months of residency training. For many states, the minimum requirement to get a license is one year, in others it is two years of residency after graduation from DO school.

Licensure as a DO in Florida, Michigan, Oklahoma, Pennsylvania, and West Virginia:

There are five states (***Florida, Michigan, Oklahoma, Pennsylvania, and West Virginia***) that require osteopathic physicians to show that they have the broad-based training of a generalist before they will be granted a license. This requirement has to be demonstrated by the completion of an **osteopathic internship**, and in some states a **transitional year (the allopathic counterpart to the osteopathic internship)**, or the equivalent which includes a month of intern-level training in medicine, surgery, obstetrics & gynaecology, and paediatrics.

Outside of these five states, the remaining US states do not have this requirement of DOs, and DOs can be licensed without the need for a osteopathic internship year, or transitional year.

What is an osteopathic internship?

An "osteopathic internship year" is also called a "traditional Rotating Year". It really is a very vestigial system of the past. It can be considered the osteopathic counterpart to the allopathic preliminary year and transitional year. It used to be the first year of post-medical school training for osteopathic graduates (equivalent to the PGY1 of the allopathic world). It is similar to the transitional year of the allopathic world.

The AOA specifically requires the clinical content to include the following in order to qualify as an osteopathic internship year:

a. Family Practice 1 month

b. Internal Medicine 2 months
c. General Surgery 1 month
d. Paediatrics 1 month
e. Women Health (OB and/or office Gyn) 1 month
f. Elective 1 month
g. Selective 4 months
h. Integrated OMM/OPP across all rotations

The osteopathic internship year is meant for:
1) Osteopathic students who is undecided regarding specialty, or
2) One requiring AOA clinical training for eventual licensure in one of the five states, or
3) One intending to match into an "advanced" PGY2 position (**some specialties require a traditional rotating year first, then you match into the program the second year - some that come to mind are PM&R, anaesthesia, radiology, dermatology)**

If you have any aspirations of practicing in "the 5 states" it makes sense to complete an AOA internship as opposed to doing a categorical/preliminary medicine year/preliminary surgery/transitional year through the allopathic match and then having to go through resolution 42.

Can I get a license without an osteopathic internship?

It is possible to be licensed in the in the five states (Florida, Michigan, Oklahoma, Pennsylvania, and West Virginia) without undergoing an osteopathic internship year through the process of applying for a **resolution 42**.

Resolution 42 is the review process for DOs who have trained in ACGME programs for their PGY1 year. Whether they are currently completing or have already completed ACGME training, DOs may be eligible for approval. With approval through resolution 42, a DO who did not go through a transitional year, or an osteopathic internship year ***may*** be licensed in those five states.

A majority of residencies match students into programs where they will complete all of their training (categorical positions). Some specialties require matching into a preliminary or transitional year (PGY-1) and a separate PGY-2 year (e.g. Radiology, Dermatology, Neurology). Some programs allow residents to enter at the PGY-1 or PGY-2 level through the match (e.g. Psychiatry).

Graduates of American osteopathic medical school may not have to worry about the osteopathic internship year as well as resolution 42 in the near future. They may soon become relics of the past in light of the AOA and ACGME merger, with complete transition of AOA residencies into ACGME accreditation by 2020.

Things you need to know about board exams and state licensure as a DO in the US:

Currently all 50 states will accept COMLEX for licensure as a DO. None of the 50 states require USMLEs (for DOs) for licensure. As a DO, the following states REQUIRES COMLEX and will not take USMLE for licensure: **California, Florida, Oklahoma, Pennsylvania, Vermont, and West Virginia.**

The following states require COMLEX if it is your first license but are willing to take USMLE if you are trying to gain licensure by state reciprocity: **Michigan, Tennessee.**

Taking the USMLE (for DO students) is only to show residency programs that you are competitive.

Some will accept COMLEX. Others will require USMLE Step 1. USMLE Step 2 is optional (since a lot of US MD students haven't taken it yet when they apply and interview) but it can help program directors at ACGME programs know your skills and strength. But it is optional and not an absolute requirement.

USMLE Step 3 is a 2-day exam to be taken once you are in residency training (doesn't have to be intern year). It is completely optional for DO students, and doesn't confer any additional advantage. I have never heard of any ACGME residency programs that require completion of USMLE series as part of their requirements (usually if they have that wording, they will accept COMLEX, since the purpose of the requirement is to make sure their residents are eligible for licensure)

Should I get licensed through the AOA or the ACGME?

Given that the COMLEX series allows the DO licensure in all fifty US states, including **California, Florida, Oklahoma, Pennsylvania, Vermont, West Virginia,** and given that completion of the USMLE series has no bearing whatsoever in relation to H1B visa sponsorship for foreign citizens who are American medical graduates, licensure through the AOA with the COMLEX series would be the path of least resistance.

Experiential pearl:

Despite the fact that I matched into family medicine in Canada, I still registered to complete my COMLEX III exam and have available the option to be licensed in the US if I so desire in the future. I chose licensure through the AOA by completion of the COMLEX series instead of the ACGME pathway and the

USMLE series. The reason is simple, 1) I had only completed my USMLE step 1 and step 2 CK, licensure through the ACGME pathway would have required me to take the USMLE step 2 CS (in which I had already paid and cancelled once), as well as the USMLE step 3 exam. It did not make sense to me to spent another 3000 US dollars to complete the USMLE series when I was only a COMLEX III exam away from AOA licensure. 2) The COMLEX III is a shorter and arguably easier exam (consisting of one day) compared to the USMLE step 3 (consisting of two days). 3) With AOA pathway to licensure, I would be accepted in all fifty states, including the states who required the complete COMLEX series for licensure. To me it was clear, I decided to take the path of least resistance for licensure, and completed my COMLEX series in its entirety.

"...hope is a good thing, maybe the best of good things, and no good thing ever dies..."

- Shawshank Redemption

Section 20:
What happens to people who go to the international schools and end up not matching in the US or Canada?

The cautionary tale "Sam":

Just a few years ago, the Caribbean, or overseas schools seemed like a good viable option for Canadians. There were numerous stories of how people with mediocre undergraduate statistics were able to attend a big four Caribbean school, who subsequently managed to match back in Canada, or at least the US in competitive specialties, like surgery, dermatology, etc. People who went through this path extol their stories

What you don't hear about are the stories of those people who failed to match into any program after graduation from these foreign institutes. The question is, what happens to these people who don't match?

One can easily find stories of success of IMGs who "made it" back in Canada for competitive specialties. But it is not nearly as easy to find stories of those who are not successful. I will give you examples of Canadians who were not successful in the match.

I have a friend, let's call him Sam. We both went to UofT for undergrad. He had a 3.5 cGPA, and 31R MCAT. He went to SGU, and for a while, everything seemed to be going right for him. He passed his step 1 USMLE, Step 2 CK USMLE. Then he became complacent. He did not study for the USMLE step 2 CS, and went into that exam expecting to pass. The pass rate for the USMLE step 2 CS is in excess of 95%. Unfortunately for Sam, he failed the Step 2 CS. However, he was able to pass the CS on the second attempt.

Sam wanted internal medicine, and he was ok with training in internal medicine in the US. He was ok with never returning home to Canada to practice. He obtained the necessary numbers of internal medicine letters of recommendation from US attendings. He was also assured that these letters of recommendation were of high calibre.

He applied to the ACGME match. In his first attempt, he applied to 150 spots, all in internal medicine, all across the US, regardless of H1B or J1 visa offered. He did not receive a single interview.

It then began to dawn on him that his USMLE step 2 CS failed attempt was a big red flag for these IM residencies, and he was refused an interview based simply for that fail.

Since he received no interviews, he decided to take up a research position in a hospital in New York City. He approached an attending in the hospital, and came to an agreement. He will help the attending publish articles for the duration of one year. In return, the attending will secure him a spot for internal medicine in that hospital for the next application cycle. In the meanwhile, he would stay on his B visitor's visa. This job was not paid.

This was when all sorts of problem started happening. After a period of one year, Sam helped the attending publish three articles in journals of cardiology. However, the attending failed to uphold his end of the bargain. He was not able to give him an internal medicine residency spot as promised. The spot instead went to a family friend who was also an IMG. What's even worse, Sam made a trip home to Canada. On the way back to NYC, he was stopped by the border guard, and he was refused to re-enter the US because of his B visitor visa status, and the fact that he was basically doing a job that was supposed to have been wage-paying.

He was only allowed back into the US after he had to pay 4000 USDs to enroll in a program of study at the local community college in NYC, and was given a student visa. In short, he paid 4000 dollars to be enrolled in college, so he can have the visa to re-enter the US to do free labour volunteer work for an attending who failed to give him a residency spot that was promised.

This attending then came up with another proposal - work for him for free for another year, and the next cycle, the attending promises that he'll get him an internal medicine residency.

Sam applied to on ERAS a second time. He again applied to 200 internal medicine spots, regardless of J1 or H1B. And again, not a single interview invitation was given to him. He called, emailed program directors all over the country, and even sat face to face with program directors in NYC for an audience. He called old attendings that he had worked with, family friends who knew program directors, all in hopes of getting an internal medicine spot. However, the meetings always ended like this:

1) He is an international medical graduate who was not a US citizen.

2) He needed visa sponsorship needed.

3) His first attempt at the USMLE step 2 CS was a fail.

For these reasons, a position in internal medicine cannot be offered.

After two failed cycles of applications to the US, Sam finally realized that his chances of matching in the US were zero.

During my US interviews, I happened to cross the state that he was residing in. To save myself from the hotel cost, I stayed over at his house and we catched up on old times as I haven't seen him in a few years. I met his parents for the first time, and they were understandably distressed about the predicament that he was in. We talked about the financial stressors and how they had to pay hundreds of dollars of interest monthly, without even touching the principle. He was noticeably downtrodden as well, and we talked about all the stressors in his life.

I distinctly remember that he was still adamant about applying to the US and matching into an internal medicine residency, despite facing the setbacks I alluded to earlier. We had a long conversation, and I tried to persuade him out of continuing with this fruitless path, and apply to CaRMS instead.

It was clear to me that failing the USMLE step 2 CS, and needing visa sponsorship were really setting him back. He may never be able to match into an ACGME residency with those two red flags on his record. However, he is a Canadian citizen, and the Canadian match does not care for the USMLE, even if you failed it.

He actually had a higher chance of matching in Canada than a 0% chance in the US match.

Sam was not entirely convinced, but at least this idea was planted into his mind. I departed the next day and continued with my own interview journey, but I continued to communicate with him, and give him advice.

A long story short, he did in fact apply to CaRMS, received one interview on the second iteration, and matched into family medicine almost three years after completing his medical degree from a Caribbean medical school.

I don't want to take any credit for this turn of events, but I hope it goes to show how changing one's perception and taking advice at vital points in one's life can have huge ramifications. I truly believe that ***you***, the reader, are in a similar position as my friend Sam. The choices you make now will have consequences that you will never foresee.

My friend Sam had choices when he was back in undergrad. But a series of arguably bad choices led him to the predicament that he was in. He could have waited and applied to the US, he could have taken additional courses in undergrad to improve his cGPA, but he rashly chose to go to the Caribbean with minimal research into what he was getting himself into. Although he matched three years after graduation, I consider him one of the lucky ones. He ***matched***. There are countless other graduates of international medical schools who end up never matching into any residency program.

Unable to find a residency but needing to pay the bills, many IMGs are going back to school to train as **physician assistants (PA)**. This would mean more tuition, and two additional years of training. A foreign medical graduate cannot simply bypass the courses of a PA program, they have to start from scratch (1).

In my opinion, having to go into more debt by becoming a physician assistant in order to make ends meet because you could not match into a residency program, while owing four years of medical school debt on top would be the absolute worst case scenario. Let's not forget that having to go through two more years of schooling for things that you should have known already from medical school is adding further insult to injury.

Bottom line:

Caribbean medical schools and foreign medical schools were designed first and foremost for Americans who have an easier time matching in America by virtue of having American citizenship. It was never really designed for Canadians. There was a time when non-US citizen IMGs matched into US residency programs with relative ease, but it appears this time has passed.

References:

(1) HealthforceOntario - PA update. Fall 2008. https://fhs.mcmaster.ca/physicianassistant/documents/200810PA-Project-UpdateOntario.pdf Accessed January 25th 2017.

"Do not go where the path may lead, go instead where there is no path and leave a trail."

- Ralph Waldo Emerson

Section 21:
A toast to your success!

What is the future of osteopathic medicine in Canada over the next 5-10 years?

One of the major problems facing the profession was a chronic shortage of US trained DOs who came back to Canada. As such, there really is no brand recognition in Canada for US DOs, as the non-doctor variety of DOs still outnumber US trained DOs.

This is starting to change with our increasing matriculation rates over the past 3 years. There are now approximately 60 Canadians matriculating at American osteopathic medical schools every year. We hope that with passing time, more Canadians will matriculate at US DO schools, and then subsequently make their way back to Canada.

Major changes have recently occurred in Saskatchewan and Prince Edward Island. For the longest time, these were the last two remaining Canadian provinces that did not allow for a USDO to receive full licensure. This changed in 2016 when these two provinces updated their policy to allow US trained

DOs full licensure (1, 2, 3). It took many years, but **as of 2017, US trained DOs have full and unrestricted practice rights in all of Canada**.

References:

(1)http://www.osteopathic.ca/Documents/Osteopathic%20Practice%20in%20Canada,%20Dec%202016.pdf
Accessed January 26th 2017

(2)http://cpspei.ca/wp-content/uploads/2015/08/REGULATIONS-FOR-PEI-Approved-Changes-as-of-May-12014.pdf
Accessed January 26th 2017

(3)https://www.cps.sk.ca/imis/Documents/Legislation/Legislation/Regulatory%20Bylaws%20-%20August%202015.pdf
Accessed January 26th 2017

What does the future hold for IMGs?

When it comes to health care policy, Canada is a fairly conservative country. It is generally very difficult for IMGs and CSAs to match into Canadian residency programs. The difficult path of IMGs and CSAs will probably remain the same for the foreseeable future.

In the US, the match rate for non-US citizens will probably become worse, owing to the **rapid expansion of both MD and DO schools**, either through brand new schools or new branch campuses. Due to the domestic expansion in the US, the number of applicants competing for the limited (but still rising!) number of US funded residency spots is increasing each year. There is a real fear among the medical student population that there might come a day when the ratio of the number of residency spots available to each US graduate will approach one to one (for the time being, there are still more residency spots than there are candidates willing to take them).

The American Osteopathic Association (AOA) recently passed a resolution in 2014 advocating for federal legislation to allow U.S. graduates first pick at U.S. residency positions. The full article is called "**House supports offering residency positions to US med school grads first**" and was first published in July 2014. The following is an excerpt.

"...the AOA House of Delegates passed a resolution calling for the profession to advocate for federal legislation to allow U.S. medical school graduates to lay first claims on U.S. residency positions.

Members of the New York State Osteopathic Medical Society (NYSOMS), which submitted the resolution, believe that ***the nation's residency positions should first be offered to graduates of U.S. medical schools before international medical graduates (IMGs) can secure them.****"*

The age where Canadians can obtain international medical education then match into US residency programs with relative ease is rapidly coming to an end, if it's not already over. Due to a combination of limited GME, massive expansion of domestic MD and DO schools in the US, IMGs will be the first to feel the pinch of the new paradigm.

The route of least resistance to residency training for non-US citizen IMGs was ACGME residency programs in the US. There is no other country in this world who has the capacity to absorb the number of IMGs requiring residency training as the US. With recent and anticipated changes, the path of foreign citizens who are IMGs planning to match into the US is becoming more and more difficult.

Countries such as Australia, Ireland, England, European Union countries may allow foreign citizens to study medicine in their medical schools, but they rarely if ever allow the same foreign students to stay after graduation to pursue graduate medical education. For these non-US countries, they simply are not set up, nor are they willing to absorb foreign citizens for postgraduate medical education.

To adapt to the changing times, the smart applicant should do whatever they can to become an AMG, no matter the MD vs. DO distinction.

Do I have to practice OMM as a DO?

OMM will always be a part of your professional title as an osteopathic physician. People with enough knowledge will ask you about OMM, residencies (in the US) will assume you know OMM. If you match back home in Canada, the provincial colleges might even invite you to give a talk about OMM!

A lot of osteopathic physicians are "osteopathic" in name only. Sure, they have passed all the COMLEX related exams, some even are licensed through the AOA, yet they do not do any OMM in their practice. One of the most common reasons is inability to bill insurance (in the US), thereby forcing the provider to charge cash for any OMM therapy.

On the flip side there are DOs who absolutely love OMM, and their entire practice is solely dedicated to treatment modalities involving OMM. This is most popular with family physicians, and family medicine practices dedicated to OMM.

In the end, it is really up to you if you value OMM, and will incorporate that into your practice. No one will force you to incorporate or not incorporate OMM treatment on your patients.

References:

(1)http://thedo.osteopathic.org/2014/07/house-supports-offering-residency-slots-us-med-school-grads-first/#comment-10393571

Accessed January 20th, 2017.

Final Thoughts:

This book is a summary of my experiences attending medical school and living in the United States for four years. Hopefully, the reader can replicate the success I have had on the interview trail and in entering the medical profession. **For the pre-meds reading this, you owe it to yourself to become an AMG (either a US MD or US DO) in order to maximize your interview chances and residency match rate.** Going to medical school is the easy part. There are institutions out there that will accept anyone to medical school if they are willing to pay. The point of medical education is not to simply get into a medical school, it is to match into a residency program ***after*** medical school. With the medical education climate being what it is, the risks of becoming an IMG or CSA should be weighed against the benefits.

Going to medical school changed my future and it changed me. I learned that I had to create the future for myself or others will do it for me. I learned that we have to take care of each other because if we don't, no one will. I learned that creativity and strength can come from the most unlikely of places. Most important though, I learned that for people dedicated to the pursuit of medicine, despite personal setbacks, there can always be new beginnings and happy conclusions.

Appendix:
Personal Statements

The following are personal statements that I used for the 2014 CaRMS and NRMP match for family medicine residency. I have included the question prompts and the exact responses I submitted.

Western University personal statement:

*A personal letter, addressed to Western's Resident Recruitment Committee, is required (word count of **600 - 800**). You MUST address all of the following questions in your letter:*

- *Why did you choose Family Medicine at Western?*
- ***What are your career plans and what aspects of our program will be particularly helpful to you in those plans?***
- *As a physician,* ***how have patient experiences of illness influenced you****?*

Three and a half years ago, I left my home in Toronto Canada, my family, my friends, and the comfortable life I had to pursue a dream in America. I started a new life for myself, and started medical school in California. The transition was at times difficult, and I always thought about Canada, my home, and the people I left behind. I vowed that one day, I would come back home, and to serve as a physician in my homeland.

My desire to pursue family medicine spans many years. I grew up in a country that had no concept of family medicine and I witnessed firsthand how the lack of a family physician affected my family and the community at large. My grandmother suffered from depression, yet no one recognized the signs and symptoms of this all too common condition. In hindsight, a simple series of screening questions pertaining to her mood, energy, sleep, concentration, and thoughts of hurting herself would have made the diagnosis. Unfortunately, in the nineteen nineties, regular care under a family physician was simply not a part of the healthcare model - rather, people would attempt to manage their own illnesses until they became severe enough to warrant a visit to see a specialist. It is with a great deal of regret that I look back on the lack of appropriate care available to my grandmother, who sadly took her own life as a result of her depression.

During my clerkship years in the US, I often encountered uninsured or poorly insured Americans not receiving adequate care. One patient who had the strongest impact on me was a young Hispanic woman in her early thirties who was already walking with a cane. It turned out that this woman has had poorly controlled type 2 diabetes for a number of years, and she became a crippled due to her uncontrolled diabetes. Her blood sugar was usually two to three times higher than the normal range. In addition to personal financial issues, this woman's insurance did not grant her access to a regular family doctor. She could not afford an insulin pump. Her idea of health maintenance was going to the emergency room whenever she has severe abdominal pain due to her uncontrolled diabetes.

Lay people's lack of understanding of the basic steps necessary to take care of themselves as well as their inability to recognize serious maladies highlights the need for family physicians worldwide. Without a family physician taking care of my family, I came to see preventable tragedies continue towards their unfortunate conclusions - things that a family doctor could have easily picked up. Having experienced these things in my family, I vowed that I would become a family doctor so that I may help others avoid the pain and suffering of these all too common conditions. **While in the U.S., I also came to see the dark side of a system where people could not afford health care - things that would not have happened in Canada with**

our universal health care. Having seen the dark side of US health care, I wish to choose Western University because I wish to return to Ontario, to return to a system of universal health care and to serve the community where I spent my adolescence. I grew up travelling the world. I spent my childhood in Asia and Europe, became an adolescent and young man in Southern Ontario, and finally went to sunny California for medical school. Having travelled greatly, I wish to be ready for family medicine anywhere in Canada and the world. Western University has a diverse array of training settings spanning the spectrum from urban to rural. From the residents I have encountered thus far, my understanding is that family medicine residents who gain the broadest skills commonly have done at least part of their training in more rural settings. It is my wish to do at least a part of my training in a more rural setting. I have no doubt that the family medicine program at Western University will adequately prepare me for family medicine anywhere in Canada and beyond.

Medicine is a lifelong learning process - the key is to keep an inquisitive mind, and to seek out learning opportunities whenever they arise. This was the case in med school, it will be the case in residency, and it will continue to be the case when I become a practicing physician. In five years time, I see myself continuing on a journey of lifelong learning, and I will continue to be a self-made student trying to learn and to improve in this art of medicine. My career goals are to be a practicing family physician out in the community with a thriving practice, and a respected member of the community. I wish to be an attending and mentor to the next wave of

medical students, helping them in their journey to become physicians.

NOSM - Personal Letter

The personal letter (maximum 2 pages) should focus on the following:

1) Experiences that led to your interest in Family Medicine;

2) Aspects of the NOSM Family Medicine RoCS program that interest you;

3) Personal qualities that make you an ideal candidate for practice in Northern settings;

4) How you anticipate this program will assist you in becoming an excellent Family Physician;

5) Your greatest challenge if you are accepted into this program

Three and a half years ago, I left my home in Canada, my family, my friends, and the comfortable life I had to pursue a dream in America. I started a new life for myself, and started medical school in California. The transition was at times difficult, and I always thought about Canada, my home, and the people I left behind. I vowed that one day, I would come back home, and to serve as a physician in my homeland.

My desire to pursue family medicine spans many years. I grew up in a country that had no concept of family medicine and I witnessed firsthand how the lack of a family physician affected my family and the community at large. My grandmother suffered from depression, yet no one recognized the signs and symptoms of this all too common condition. In hindsight, a simple series of screening questions pertaining to her mood, energy, sleep, concentration, and thoughts of hurting herself would have made the diagnosis. Unfortunately, in the nineteen nineties, regular care under a family physician was simply not a part of the healthcare model - rather, people would attempt to manage their own illnesses until they became severe enough to warrant a visit to see a specialist. It is with a great deal of regret that I look back on the lack of appropriate care available to my grandmother, who sadly took her own life as a result of her depression.

Lay people's lack of understanding of the basic steps necessary to take care of themselves as well as their inability to recognize serious maladies highlights the need for family physicians worldwide. Without a family physician taking care of my family, I came to see preventable tragedies continue towards their unfortunate conclusions - things that a family doctor could have easily picked up. Having experienced these things, I vowed that I would become a family doctor so that I may help others avoid the pain and suffering of these all too common conditions.

Teamwork, self-directed learning, and finding the right balance between professional life and personal life are necessities of being a successful family medicine resident in the present, and a practicing family medicine physician in the future. I possess these traits. During my time in school, I felt comfortable and excelled with self-directed learning. In medical school, the curriculum was problem-based, and the need for self-directed learning only increased. Teamwork is also an integral part of the residency program experience, and I am well prepared to function effectively in a team setting. I have had plentiful experiences working with students from the various other branches of health care during my medical education, including nurses, PAs, dentists, and even veterinarians. Finding a balance between school and personal life is an extremely difficult task, and for this reason I trained both the mind and the body during med school. With each week of school work, I would set scheduled times for physical exercise in the local gym, while working hard to keep relationships with friends and family alive, even when times were hectic. The result was a fair compromise between the rigors of a med school curriculum, and the human yearning for social contact.

I grew up travelling the world. I spent my childhood in Asia and Europe, became an adolescent and young man in Ontario, and finally went to sunny California for medical school. After four years in the US Southwest, I think it is time for me to come home to Canada, and to experience life in Northern Ontario. I have always wanted to experience the great outdoors. I have experienced the scorching heat of the California desert, and now I want to contrast that experience with the cooler climate of Northern Ontario. I think now is the perfect time for me to make this transition, and to start a new life for myself.

My greatest regret during medical school was not being able to do as many procedures as I had liked during clinical clerkship. I am very impressed and intrigued by NOSM's resident tracking system that will keep track of the exact number and types of procedures that I have done. It appears that at NOSM, I will be adequately trained in the way of procedures.

One of my greatest fears as a medical student was being thrown into a situation in which I had absolutely no idea what to do. From the residents I have encountered thus far, my understanding is that family medicine residents who gain the broadest skills commonly have done at least part of their training in more rural settings. I anticipate that the family medicine program at NOSM will prepare me for practice in any community, especially in rural and remote areas. With the skills that I have gained in this program, I am confident that I will practice with confidence and distinction in any setting in Canada. Many challenges lie ahead if I am selected at NOSM - adjusting to life as a resident, the long hours of training ahead, even adjustment to the cooler climate as I have grown accustomed to the desert heat. However, as I have always done in the past when moving to a new environment, I have no doubt in my abilities to adapt quickly and to thrive in my new home.

Medicine is a lifelong learning process - the key is to keep an inquisitive mind, and to seek out learning opportunities whenever they arise. This was the case in med school, it will be the case in residency, and it will continue to be the case when I become a practicing physician. In five years time, I see myself continuing on a journey of lifelong learning, and I will continue to be a self-made student trying to learn and to improve in this art of medicine. My career goals are to be a practicing family physician out in the community with a thriving practice, and a respected member of the community. I wish to be an attending and mentor to medical students who just started on their careers. And I wish to be a guide to the next wave of medical students, helping them in their journey to become physicians.

<u>Queen's Personal Letter</u>

The personal letter is a crucial part of your CaRMS application. Your letter should be approximately 500 words and should ***focus on you as an individual, and your interest in Family Medicine****.*

In your personal letter, indicate why you feel that Queen's Family Medicine Program would be a good match for you.

We are particularly interested in your life experiences and goals that you feel make you an appropriate candidate for our program.

Three and a half years ago, I left my home in Toronto Canada, my family, my friends, and the comfortable life I had to pursue a dream in America. I started a new life for myself, and started medical school in California. The transition was at times difficult, and I always thought about Canada, my home, and the people I left behind. I vowed that one day, I would come back home, and to serve as a physician in my homeland.

My desire to pursue family medicine spans many years. I grew up in a country that had no concept of family medicine and I witnessed firsthand how the lack of a family physician affected my family and the community at large. My grandmother suffered from depression, yet no one recognized the signs and symptoms of this all too common condition. In hindsight, a simple series of screening questions pertaining to her mood, energy, sleep, concentration, and thoughts of hurting herself would have made the diagnosis. Unfortunately, in the nineteen nineties, regular care under a family physician was simply not a part of the healthcare model - rather, people would attempt to manage their own illnesses until they became severe enough to warrant a visit to see a specialist. It is with a great deal of regret that I look back on the lack of appropriate care available to my grandmother, who sadly took her own life as a result of her depression.

Lay people's lack of understanding of the basic steps necessary to take care of themselves as well as their inability to recognize serious maladies highlights the need for family physicians worldwide. Without a family physician taking care of my family, I came to see preventable tragedies continue towards their unfortunate conclusions - things that a family doctor could have easily picked up. Having experienced these things, I vowed that I would become a family doctor so that I may help others avoid the pain and suffering of these all too common conditions.

I grew up travelling the world. I spent my childhood in Asia and Europe, became an adolescent and young man in Southern Ontario, and finally went to sunny California for medical school. I wish to be ready for family medicine anywhere in the world. I have no doubt that the family medicine program at Queen's University will adequately prepare me for that task.

Medicine is a lifelong learning process - the key is to keep an inquisitive mind, and to seek out learning opportunities whenever they arise. This was the case in med school, it will be the case in residency, and it will continue to be the case when I become a practicing physician. In five years time, I see myself continuing on a journey of lifelong learning, and I will continue to be a self-made student trying to learn and to improve in this art of medicine. My career goals are to be a practicing family physician out in the community with a thriving practice, and a respected member of the community. I wish to be an attending and mentor to the next wave of

medical students, helping them in their journey to become physicians.

McGill - Personal Letter

A personal letter is required. Topics to be covered **might include**:

- What you would like us to know about you in order to fully consider your application,
- **Brief biographical sketch,**
- **Reason for career choice of family medicine,**
- **Personal attributes that you possess that fit you for this career,**
- Pursuits outside of medicine,
- **Future plans,**
- Why you are interested in training at McGill University.
- It is important that you demonstrate your understanding of Family Medicine discipline within this letter.

It is suggested that this letter not be any longer than 500 words.

Three and a half years ago, I left my home in Canada, my family, my friends, and the comfortable life I had to pursue a dream in America. I started a new life for myself, and started medical school in California. The transition was at times difficult, and I always thought about Canada, my home, and the people I left behind. I vowed that one day, I would come back home, and to serve as a physician in my homeland.

My desire to pursue family medicine spans many years. I grew up in a country that had no concept of family medicine and I witnessed firsthand how the lack of a family physician affected my family and the community at large. My grandmother suffered from depression, yet no one recognized the signs and symptoms of this all too common condition. In hindsight, a simple series of screening questions pertaining to her mood, energy, sleep, concentration, and thoughts of hurting herself would have made the diagnosis. Unfortunately, in the nineteen nineties, regular care under a family physician was simply not a part of the healthcare model - rather, people would attempt to manage their own illnesses until they became severe enough to warrant a visit to see a specialist. It is with a great deal of regret that I look back on the lack of appropriate care available to my grandmother, who sadly took her own life as a result of her depression.

Lay people's lack of understanding of the basic steps necessary to take care of themselves as well as their inability to recognize serious maladies highlights the need for family physicians worldwide. Without a family physician taking care of my family, I came to see preventable tragedies continue towards their unfortunate conclusions - things that a family doctor could have easily picked up. Having experienced these things, I vowed that I would become a family doctor so that I may help others avoid the pain and suffering of these all too common conditions.

Medicine is a lifelong learning process - the key is to keep an inquisitive mind, and to seek out learning opportunities whenever they arise. This was the case in medical school, it will be the case in residency, and it will continue to be the case when I become a practicing physician. In five years time, I see myself continuing on a journey of lifelong learning, and I will continue to be a self-made student trying to learn and to improve in this art of medicine. My career goals are to be a practicing family physician out in the community with a thriving practice, and a respected member of the community. I wish to be an attending and mentor to the next wave of

medical students, helping them in their journey to become physicians.

McMaster - Personal statement

McMaster Family Medicine has a centralized admissions process requiring only one personal letter regardless of the number of applications you submit to the various streams in our program. The personal letter (maximum 1000 words and in paragraph format) must answer each of the following questions:

- **Why have you chosen a career in Family Medicine and what experiences have led you to this career choice?**
- Why are you applying to the program at McMaster?
- Which **personal qualities** do you think are critical to a family physician and how do you measure up? - patience
- **What are your personal and professional goals for the future?**
- Please tell us anything else that you feel is important to your application to our program.

Three and a half years ago, I left my home in Toronto Canada, my family, my friends, and the comfortable life I had to pursue a dream in America. I started a new life for myself, and started medical school in California. The transition was at times difficult, and I always thought about Canada, my home, and the people I left behind. I vowed that one day, I would come back home, and to serve as a physician in my homeland. Throughout my medical education, I had the opportunity to meet several Canadian residents and fellows from McMaster. Their opinions about McMaster's family medicine program were unanimous: this was a place that "made happy residents". It is understood that residency is a difficult time, so I put a great deal of value in personal anecdotes that extol the virtues of graduate medical education programs. It is this reputation for quality combined with my desire to return to Canada that make McMaster's family medicine program my primary choice for residency.

My desire to pursue family medicine spans many years. I grew up in a country that had no concept of family medicine and I witnessed firsthand how the lack of a family physician affected my family and the community at large. My grandmother suffered from depression, yet no one recognized the signs and symptoms of this all too common condition. In hindsight, a simple series of screening questions pertaining to her mood, energy, sleep, concentration, and thoughts of hurting herself would have made the diagnosis. Unfortunately, in the nineteen nineties, regular care under a family physician was simply not a part of the healthcare model - rather, people would attempt to manage their own illnesses until they became severe enough to warrant a visit to see a specialist. It is with a great deal of regret that I look back on the lack of appropriate care available to my grandmother, who sadly took her own life as a result of her depression.

On another occasion, I once again witnessed the consequences of lacking a regular family physician when visiting my grandfather after almost a decade abroad. He had gout, and complained of an excruciating pain coming from his foot, near the great toe. Yet when asked what he was going to do for this pain, all he did was drink a concoction of traditional Chinese herbal medicine with questionable effect. He did not visit a doctor of western medicine and he had not done so for many years. By the time he did visit a hospital, it was discovered that his blood uric acid levels was extremely high, and that his kidneys had severely diminished function.

Lay people's lack of understanding of the basic steps necessary to take care of themselves as well as their inability to recognize serious maladies highlights the need for family physicians worldwide. Without a family physician taking care of my family, I came to see preventable tragedies continue towards their unfortunate conclusions - things that a family doctor could have easily picked up. Having experienced these things, I vowed that I would become a family doctor so that I may help others avoid the pain and suffering of these all too common conditions.

Teamwork, self-directed learning, and finding the right balance between professional life and personal life are necessities of being a successful family medicine resident in the present, and a practicing family medicine physician in the future. I believe that I possess many of these traits. During my time in school, I felt comfortable and excelled with self-directed learning. In medical school, the curriculum was problem-based, and the need for self-directed learning only increased. Teamwork is also an integral part of the residency program experience, and I am well prepared to function effectively in a team setting. I have had plentiful experiences working with students from the various other branches of health care during my medical education, including nurses, PAs, dentists, and even veterinarians. Finding a balance between school and personal life is an extremely difficult task, and for this reason I trained both the mind and the body during med school. With each week of school work, I would set scheduled times for physical exercise in the local gym, while working hard to keep relationships with friends and family alive, even when times were hectic. The result was a fair compromise between the rigors of a med school curriculum, and the human yearning for social contact.

Medicine is a lifelong learning process - the key is to keep an inquisitive mind, and to seek out learning opportunities whenever they arise. This was the case in med school, it will be the case in residency, and it will continue to be the case when I become a practicing physician. In five years time, I see myself continuing on a journey of lifelong learning, and I will continue to be a self-made student trying to learn and to improve in this art of medicine. My career goals are to be a practicing family physician out in the community with a thriving practice, and a respected member of the community. I wish to be an attending and mentor to medical students who just started on their careers. And I wish to be a guide to the next wave of medical students, helping them in their journey to become physicians.

Ottawa - Personal statement

A personal letter, that should explain why you have chosen family medicine as your professional career, as well as experiences in your past that have led you to choose this specialty. You should also enumerate personal attributes you possess that fit you for this career.

My desire to pursue family medicine spans many years. I grew up in a country that had no concept of family medicine and I witnessed firsthand how the lack of a family physician affected my family and the community at large. My grandmother suffered from depression, yet no one recognized the signs and symptoms of this all too common condition. In hindsight, a simple series of screening questions pertaining to her mood, energy, sleep, concentration, and thoughts of hurting herself would have made the diagnosis. Unfortunately, in the nineteen nineties, regular care under a family physician was simply not a part of the healthcare model - rather, people would attempt to manage their own illnesses until they became severe enough to warrant a visit to see a specialist. It is with a great deal of regret that I look back on the lack of appropriate care available to my grandmother, who sadly took her own life as a result of her depression.

On another occasion, I once again witnessed the consequences of lacking a regular family physician when visiting my grandfather after almost a decade abroad. He had gout, and complained of an excruciating pain coming from his foot, near the great toe. Yet when asked what he was going to do for this pain, all he did was drink a concoction of traditional Chinese herbal medicine with questionable effect. He did not visit a doctor of western medicine and he had not done so for many years. By the time he did visit a hospital, it was discovered that his blood uric acid levels was extremely high, and that his kidneys had severely diminished function.

Lay people's lack of understanding of the basic steps necessary to take care of themselves as well as their inability to recognize serious maladies highlights the need for family physicians worldwide. Without a family physician taking care of my family, I came to see preventable tragedies continue towards their unfortunate conclusions - things that a family doctor could have easily picked up. Having experienced these things, I vowed that I would become a family doctor so that I may help others avoid the pain and suffering of these all too common conditions.

Teamwork, self-directed learning, and finding the right balance between professional life and personal life are necessities of being a successful family medicine resident in the present, and a practicing family medicine physician in the future. I believe that I possess many of these traits. During my time in school, I felt comfortable and excelled with self-directed learning. In medical school, the curriculum was problem-based, and the need for self-directed learning only increased. Teamwork is also an integral part of the residency program experience, and I am well prepared to function effectively in a team setting. I have had plentiful experiences working with students from the various other branches of health care during my medical education, including nurses, PAs, dentists, and even veterinarians. Finding a balance between school and personal life is an extremely difficult task, and for this reason I trained both the mind and the body during med school. With each week of school work, I would set scheduled times for physical exercise in the local gym, while working hard to keep relationships with friends and family alive, even when times were hectic. The result was a fair compromise between the rigors of a med school curriculum, and the human yearning for social contact.

Medicine is a lifelong learning process - the key is to keep an inquisitive mind, and to seek out learning opportunities whenever they arise. This was the case in med school, it will be the case in residency, and it will continue to be the case when I become a practicing physician. In five years time, I see myself continuing on a journey of lifelong learning, and I will continue to be a self-made student trying to learn and to improve in this art of medicine. My career goals are to be a practicing family physician out in the community with a thriving practice, and a respected member of the community. I wish to be an attending and mentor to medical students who just started on their careers. And I wish to be a guide to the next wave of medical students, helping them in their journey to become physicians.

Kaiser Permanente Personal statement

What am I looking for in a residency program?
Why am I interested in the field I have chosen?
What are my professional goals in the field I have chosen?

Kaiser Permanente is a well known name that is recognized far and wide. Even in jurisdictions outside the US, such as Canada (my home), Kaiser's reputation precedes them, and I often hear the "Kaiser" name being whispered by Canadian doctors and medical students. It is well known that Kaiser Permanente medical training positions are competitive, attracting the best and brightest people in their respective fields. Kaiser Permanente is one of the few organizations that is willing to sponsor visas for graduate medical education to train the next generation of foreign citizens. As a foreign citizen studying in a US medical school, I am required to be under specific visas during my continued medical education into residency. Because of Kaiser's history of facilitating such accommodations for foreign citizens of US medical schools and their clear reputation and quality of care, it is my wish to spent my time in this organization and to learn from the best in the medical field.

My desire to pursue family medicine spans many years, which are dotted with personal experiences and family tragedies. I grew up in a country that had no concept of family medicine and I witnessed firsthand how the lack of a family physician affected my family and the community at large. My grandmother suffered from depression, yet no one recognized the signs and symptoms of this all too common condition. In hindsight, a simple series of screening questions pertaining to her mood, energy, sleep, concentration, and thoughts of hurting herself would have made the diagnosis. Unfortunately, in the nineteen nineties, regular care under a family physician was simply not a part of the healthcare model - rather, people would attempt to manage their own illnesses until they became severe enough to warrant a visit to see a specialist. It is with a great deal of regret that I look back on the lack of appropriate care available to my grandmother, who sadly took her own life as a result of her depression.

On another occasion, I once again witnessed the consequences of lacking a regular family physician when visiting my grandfather after almost a decade abroad. He had gout, and complained of an excruciating pain coming from his foot, near the great toe. Yet when asked what he was going to do for this pain, all he did was drink a concoction of traditional Chinese herbal medicine with questionable effect. He did not visit a doctor of western medicine and he had not done so for many years. By the time he did visit a hospital, it was discovered that his blood uric acid levels was extremely high, and that his kidneys had severely diminished function.

Lay people's lack of understanding of medicine and their lack of knowledge of the basic steps necessary to take care of themselves highlights the need for a regular family physician in communities worldwide. Without a family physician taking care of my family, I came to see preventable tragedies continue towards their unfortunate conclusions - things that a family doctor could have easily picked up. Having experienced these things, I vowed that I would become a family doctor so that I may help others avoid the pain and suffering of these all too common conditions.

Teamwork, self-directed learning, and finding the right balance between professional life and personal life are necessities of being a successful family medicine resident in the present, and a practicing family medicine physician in the future. I believe that I possess many of these traits. During my time in school, I felt comfortable and excelled with self-directed learning. In medical school, the curriculum was problem-based, and the need for self-directed learning only increased. Teamwork is also an integral part of the residency program experience, and I am well prepared to function effectively in a team setting. I have had plentiful experiences working with students from the various other branches of health care during my medical education, including nurses, PAs, dentists, and even veterinarians. Finding a balance between school and personal life is an extremely difficult task, and for this reason I trained both the mind and the body during med school. With each week of school work, I would set scheduled times for physical exercise in the local gym, while working hard to keep relationships with friends and family alive, even when times were hectic. The result was a fair compromise between the rigors of a med school curriculum, and the human yearning for social contact.

Medicine is a lifelong learning process - the key is to keep an inquisitive mind, and to seek out learning opportunities whenever they arise. This was the case in med school, it will be the case in residency, and it will continue to be the case when I become a practicing physician. In five years time, I see myself continuing on a journey of lifelong learning, and I will continue to be a self-made student trying to learn and to improve in this art of medicine. My career goals are to be a practicing family physician out in the community with a thriving practice, and a respected member of the community. I wish to be an attending and mentor to medical students who just started on their careers. And I wish to be a guide to the next wave of medical students, helping them in their journey to become physicians.

Manufactured by Amazon.ca
Bolton, ON

12791379R00118